SERVING AWAY FROM HOME

How Deployments Influence Reenlistment

JAMES HOSEK   MARK TOTTEN

Prepared for the

Office of the Secretary of Defense

National Defense Research Institute

RAND

The research described in this report was sponsored by the Office of the Secretary of Defense (OSD). The research was conducted in RAND's National Defense Research Institute, a federally funded research and development center supported by the OSD, the Joint Staff, the unified commands, and the defense agencies under Contract DASW01-01-C-0004.

Library of Congress Cataloging-in-Publication Data

Hosek, James R.
    Serving away from home : how deployments influence reenlistment / James R.
Hosek, Mark Totten.
      p. cm.
    "MR-1594."
    Includes bibliographical references.
    ISBN 0-8330-3215-1
    1. United States—Armed Forces—Recruiting, enlistment, etc. 2. United
States—Armed Forces—Foreign service. I. Totten, Mark, 1969– II.Title.

UB323 .H6736 2002
355.2'2—dc21

2002068216

RAND is a nonprofit institution that helps improve policy and decisionmaking through research and analysis. RAND® is a registered trademark. RAND's publications do not necessarily reflect the opinions or policies of its research sponsors.

Published 2002 by RAND
1700 Main Street, P.O. Box 2138, Santa Monica, CA 90407-2138
1200 South Hayes Street, Arlington, VA 22202-5050
201 North Craig Street, Suite 202, Pittsburgh, PA 15213-1516
RAND URL: http://www.rand.org/
To order RAND documents or to obtain additional information,
contact Distribution Services: Telephone: (310) 451-7002;
Fax: (310) 451-6915; Email: order@rand.org

The research in this report concerns whether deployment affects reenlistment. The relationship between deployment and reenlistment is an area of policy interest because of the high rate of deployment in the past decade and the prospect that deployment will rise even more. The report provides a conceptual framework for understanding how deployment experience can influence reenlistment behavior. It also presents empirical estimates of the effect of deployment on reenlistment. The report should be of interest to defense manpower planners, deployers, and policymakers, all of whom share a concern about the heightened pace of deployments that our nation has experienced since the end of the Cold War.

This report was prepared under the sponsorship of the Office of Special Projects and Research within the Office of the Under Secretary of Defense for Personnel and Readiness. It was prepared within the Forces and Resources Policy Center of RAND's National Defense Research Institute, a federally funded research and development center sponsored by the Office of the Secretary of Defense, the Joint Staff, the unified commands, and the defense agencies.

CONTENTS

FIGURES

CONCEPTUAL FRAMEWORK

Our research considered whether deployment affects the reenlistment of enlisted members and why. A fundamental underlying question was why past deployment should exert any influence on current reenlistment behavior. We suggest that a relationship exists because deployment enables members to learn about their preferences for deployment and about the frequency and duration of deployment.

We hypothesized that members enter military service with naive expectations about how much they will like deployment, the frequency and duration of deployment, and the variance of frequency and duration. These expectations are revised following an actual deployment experience. We described this learning mechanism as a *Bayesian updating process*. Although each deployment has its own characteristics, we hypothesized that learning occurs because deployments have common aspects—such as the separation from family and friends; the opportunity to apply training on missions, risks; the opportunity to demonstrate proficiency, resolve, and courage; as well as the possible sense of personal fulfillment. If deployment proves to be more satisfying than expected, the member revises upward his or her expected utility of remaining in service.

To demonstrate how deployment can influence reenlistment, we presented a model of the expected utility of another term in service. Higher expected utility should lead to higher reenlistment. The model depends on parameters the member can learn about from past deployment: preferences for time deployed versus time at home station, for the variance in deployments and for the variance in deployment length. Using different parameter values, we showed how expected utility may be positively related to the expected number and variance of deployments over a reasonable range of parameter values, and positively or negatively related to the expected length and variance of a deployment. The expected utility model paved the way for our empirical work, which estimated the effect of past deployment on reenlistment.

STRUCTURE OF RESEARCH

We estimated two models of deployment and reenlistment. One model treats reenlistment as a function of deployment indicators. The other model has two equations: one for reenlistment and one for the time to E-5 promotion. In this model, deployment has a direct effect on reenlistment as in the first model, but it also has an indirect effect. The indirect effect operates through the effect of deployment on time to E-5, and the effect of expected time to E-5 on reenlistment. The model allows the error terms in the promotion and reenlistment equations to be correlated, which enables the detection of unobserved factors affecting both outcomes. We estimated the models by branch of service for first- and second-term reenlistment decisions.

In the deployment/reenlistment model, we estimated two specifications of the deployment variables: a main-effect specification and full-interaction specification. In the main-effect specification, the deployment variables indicate the number of nonhostile deployments and the number of hostile deployments (i.e., deployments involving hostile duty). In the full-interaction specification, the deployment variables indicate combinations of nonhostile and hostile deployments—e.g., one nonhostile deployment and one hostile deployment. In the two-equation model, we estimated only the main-effect specification.

The data cover members facing a reenlistment decision during FY1996–FY1999. We counted deployments over a three-year period ending three months prior to the date when the member made a decision to reenlist or to leave the military. Thus, the counting period extends back to the beginning of 1993. Also, the member receives deployment pays and bears fixed and variable costs of deployment, and the deployment indicators reflect both the deployment experience and these pays and costs. Our results are conditional on the types of deployments and the deployment pays in the analysis period.

The deployment/reenlistment model treats reenlistment as a function of the member's deployment variables, education level, Armed Forces Qualification Test score category, occupational area, race/ethnicity, gender, dependency status, unemployment rate at entry, current unemployment rate, and fiscal year. The two-equation model retains the same variables in the reenlistment equation but also adds the expected time to E-5 promotion. The promotion equation includes the variables in the reenlistment equation, indicators of the member's promotion speed to E-4, and indicators of the calendar quarter when the member entered service.

FINDINGS FROM THE ONE-EQUATION MODEL OF REENLISTMENT

With few exceptions, we found that reenlistment among members who deployed was at least as high as reenlistment among members who did not deploy, and often considerably higher. When deployment had a negative effect on reenlistment, the effect was small.

For the first term, reenlistment typically rose with nonhostile deployments and did not change with respect to hostile deployments:

- In the Army, Air Force, and Marine Corps, reenlistment rose with the number of nonhostile deployments. This is consistent with expected utility increasing with the number of nonhostile deployments.

- For the Navy, reenlistment was higher among members with some deployment but did not rise with the number of nonhostile deployments. This is consistent with the idea that first-term sailors learn about nonhostile deployment from the first deployment but not from additional deployments.

- Hostile deployment typically had a small effect on reenlistment. In the main-effect specification, reenlistment changed little as the number of hostile deployments increased. This was also true in the full-interaction model for the Army and Marine Corps. However, for the Navy and Air Force, going from zero to one or from one to two hostile deployments decreased reenlistment for members with one or more nonhostile deployments. Overall, the effect of hostile deployments was small compared with that for nonhostile deployments. The finding was consistent with the idea that hostile deployments have positive and negative aspects, and that learning about these aspects, along with the receipt of deployment-related pay, leaves expected utility little changed on net.

- The full-interaction specification revealed that members with the most deployment (three or more nonhostile deployments and three or more hostile deployments) had lower reenlistment than did members with two nonhostile or two hostile deployments. This suggested that total deployment among the most-deployed was greater than these members preferred.

For the second term, reenlistment rose with nonhostile deployments and with the first and the second hostile deployment, which encompassed most members who had hostile deployment:

- Reenlistment increased with the number of nonhostile deployments. This was true for the Army, Air Force, and Marine Corps, in the first term, as well as for the Navy. Members apparently continued to learn about nonhostile deployment in their second term; most members had only one deployment or no deployment in their first term. The positive effect for the Navy suggested that deployment was more satisfying in the second term than in the first term. Second-term sailors receive career sea pay and have been trained in a rating (occupational specialty), whereas many first-term sailors did not receive career sea pay (during our study period) and began without training, serving as "general detail."

- Reenlistment increased with the number of hostile deployments up to two, which differed from the first-term results where it did not change. The increase in reenlistment may reflect the selectivity of second-term members relative to first-term members, and possibly higher satisfaction from participating in hostile deployments at a higher rank.

- Reenlistment declined somewhat for Army and Marine Corps members with three or more hostile deployments but did not for Navy or Air Force members. Still, reenlistment remained higher than for members who had no hostile deployment. The decline in reenlistment with three or more hostile deployments was consistent with the idea that the member had more time deployed than was preferred.

We used the main-effect model to predict how a 25-percent increase in episodes, all hostile, would affect reenlistment. Spreading the episodes across members at random by a Poisson process, we found that first- and second-term reenlistment would be virtually unchanged, perhaps even rising slightly.

We conducted a number of empirical excursions to test the robustness of the findings. We ran models that added months deployed as an explanatory variable. Months deployed had a negative effect on reenlistment for the Air Force, Navy, and Marine Corps but a positive effect on reenlistment for the Army. Although the inclusion of months deployed sometimes affected the coefficients on the deployment indicator variables, on the whole the effect of deployment (through the indictor *and* months variables) remained much the same. We showed in the conceptual modeling that either effect, negative or positive, was consistent with the expected utility model. Also, we estimated models for members with a four-year term of service and found results similar to the results for members with four-year or longer terms, which are reported above.

FINDINGS FROM THE TWO-EQUATION MODEL OF PROMOTION AND REENLISTMENT

The joint model of promotion speed and reenlistment indicated that time to E-5 was shorter with a greater number of nonhostile deployments but was little affected by the number of hostile deployments. For example, a member with two nonhostile episodes was promoted faster than a member with one nonhostile and one hostile episode, and that member was promoted faster than a member with no episodes of any kind. These patterns were present in all branches and were stronger in the Army and Air Force than they were in the Navy and Marine Corps.

Although deployment tended to reduce time to E-5, the reduction was small. Furthermore, we found that a shorter expected time to E-5 resulted in an only slightly higher reenlistment probability. Therefore, although deployment affected reenlistment via promotion speed, the pathway was minor. The presence of this indirect pathway did little to affect the direct relationship between deployment and reenlistment described above.

We found evidence of unobserved variables that affected both promotion speed and reenlistment. The evidence was in the form of a large negative correlation between the error terms in the promotion and reenlistment equations except in one case (first-term reenlistment in the Air Force). We computed the implications of this correlation: Controlling for their observed variables, members who reached E-5 faster were considerably more likely to reenlist. This relationship appeared to be strong enough to merit further research to identify the unobserved factors.

REENLISTMENT AND DEPENDENCY STATUS

We were interested in whether the relationship between deployment and reenlistment differed by a member's dependency status at the time of the reenlistment decision. For most members, having dependents meant being married and, perhaps, having some children. We focused on first-term personnel because most second-term personnel have dependents. We found that for any given number of nonhostile and hostile deployments, members with dependents typically had a *higher* reenlistment probability. Furthermore, for these members reenlistment tended to *increase* with the number of nonhostile or hostile deployments, whereas for members without dependents, it rose less rapidly for nonhostile deployments and was unchanged, or declined slightly, for hostile deployments. If we had found only a difference in reenlistment between members with and without dependents, we could attribute this to selection effects related to getting married. But we found that the difference in reenlistment varied with the *number of deployments.* We believe this reflected an unobserved factor that predisposed a member to discover that deployment was satisfying, which correlated with getting married. Compared with other members, members who married while in service presumably found the military, and its deployments, to their liking.

As mentioned, we found that the effect of nonhostile and hostile deployments on second-term reenlistment was positive. The similarity of the second-term results to those of first-term members with dependents probably reflects the selectivity of first-term reenlistment. The higher first-term reenlistment rate for members with dependents, coupled with the positive effect of deployment on reenlistment for those members, implies an overall higher reenlistment rate for members with dependents who liked deployment.

DEPLOYMENT PAYS

Deployment pays compensate for separation, danger, arduous duty, and inhospitable conditions. In effect, these pays help to reimburse the member for deployment-related costs such as making arrangements to have bills paid, possessions looked after, and responsibilities attended to during an absence for deployment. For married members, some of these costs may be shifted to the spouse, who must handle child care and household chores, often in addition to holding a job. We could not study the effect of deployment pays or costs because there was little variation in deployment pays in our study period and no data on deployment costs in our database. We suspect that deployment pays play an important role as intended by policy, but we have no empirical evidence to offer on their effect on reenlistment.

CONCLUSIONS

We found that reenlistment was higher among members who deployed compared with those who did not deploy. Reenlistment tended to rise with the number of nonhostile deployments and changed little with the number of hostile deployments. For the vast majority of members with hostile deployments, reenlistment was no lower (and sometimes was higher) than for members who did not deploy. We found that a sizeable increase in deployments, all hostile, appeared unlikely to reduce reenlistment. Finally, the results were consistent with the notion that members used their deployment experience to revise their expectations about whether they liked deployment, and this learning mechanism created a bridge between past deployment and current reenlistment decisions.

ACKNOWLEDGMENTS

We thank Teri Cholar, Michael Dove, and Robert Brandewie of the Defense Manpower Data Center for providing the data file used in our analysis. We appreciate the insightful reviews provided by RAND colleague Carole Roan Gresenz and Professor John Warner of Clemson University, and we acknowledge our debt to RAND's Michael Mattock and Stan Panis on issues concerning model estimation. We thank CMDR Kevin Harkins, Office of Compensation, OSD(P&R), for advice regarding deployment pays. Our project sponsor, Dr. Curtis Gilroy, Director of Office of Special Projects and Research, OSD (P&R), offered helpful comments at several stages of this research and was steadfast in his support of the project. We benefited from the opportunity to present this research at a conference on personnel tempo and readiness, convened in October 2001 at the request of Dr. David Chu, Under Secretary of Defense for Personnel and Readiness. We are grateful to Susan Everingham, Director of NDRI's Forces and Resources Policy Center at RAND, for her support and commitment to the project's completion.

ABBREVIATIONS

AFQT	Armed Forces Qualification Test
BAS	Basic Allowance for Subsistence
CS	Composite score
DMDC	Defense Manpower Data Center
ETS	Expiration of term of service
FSA	Family Separation Allowance
FY	Fiscal year
GAO	General Accounting Office
GED	General Equivalency Diploma
HFP	Hostile Fire/Imminent Danger Pay
OSD(P&R)	Office of the Secretary of Defense for Readiness and Personnel
PARS	Personnel advancement requirements
PERSTEMPO	Personnel tempo
PFE	Promotion fitness examination
PNA	Pass-not-advanced
SD	Standard deviation
SEPRATS	Separate Rations
SKT	Specialty knowledge test

| STEP | Stripes for exceptional performance |
| WAPS | Weighted airman promotion system |

Chapter One

INTRODUCTION

Two changes loom over others in defining the defense manpower environment of the 1990s. The unexpected end of the Cold War led to a reduction in the size of the active-duty military force from 2.1 million to 1.4 million personnel. At the same time, U.S. national security strategy was increasingly directed toward actions intended to shape the security of the post–Cold War world, support the development of democratic institutions, and promote trade and commercial relations. The change in strategy led to the growing involvement of U.S. forces in a wide variety of humanitarian, disaster relief, peacemaking, and peacekeeping operations, as well as new roles in border patrol and interdiction in the war against drugs. Thus, the United States found itself with a smaller active-duty force that was more frequently used in operations than had been the case during the Cold War, and the operations were highly diverse. In addition, the need to be ready for major theater war, although reduced, had not disappeared. U.S. forces engaged in Gulf War operations in 1990–1991 and are engaged in the current war against terrorism, which began in late 2001. The need to be ready for major theater war, the expanded role of peacetime operations, and actual wars themselves combined to make a heightened pace of military activity—and intense utilization of military personnel—the new norm. The recent rise of terrorism and threats against U.S. interests has reinforced this change.

Our report focuses on the relationship between the deployment and reenlistment of enlisted personnel. The major policy issue here is whether the more-intense utilization of personnel hurts retention and readiness. We concentrate on the important subset of deployments that involve long separation or hostile duty. If such deployments reduce reenlistment, units may face manning shortfalls and higher personnel turnover and therefore may have difficulty maintaining readiness. Reduced reenlistment may also increase recruiting requirements and entail more personnel and resources in recruiting, further reducing the personnel and resources available to maintain unit readiness. Furthermore, lower reenlistment could be a negative signal to prospective recruits about the satisfaction from service in the military, making it harder for the services to meet their recruiting goals. If such deployments increase reenlistment, however, positive effects may occur: higher readiness, less turnover, lower recruiting requirements, fewer personnel and resources engaged in recruiting, and a positive signal to recruit prospects.

There are broad signs to support the common view that deployments hurt retention. The number of deployments rose in the 1990s, and many involved hostile duty. By the late 1990s, the services reported that retention had become more difficult. We can see evidence of this in Figure 1.1, which plots information about deployment and reenlistment for first-term enlisted members by service for FY1996–FY1999. For each fiscal year, we counted long and hostile deployments in a three-year period preceding the fiscal year. (The definitions of deployment and reenlistment are provided in Chapter Three.) As the figure shows, the Army and the Air Force experienced a significant increase in the percentage of personnel who had at least one episode of deployment. The increase in this percentage was largely driven by the increase in hostile episodes; the second set of bars shows an increase in the percentage of members who had at least one deployment involving hostile duty. The third set of bars shows our estimate of the reenlistment rate. We see that as the percentage of soldiers and airmen with deployment rose, the first-term reenlistment rate declined, as the common view suggests.

The patterns for sailors and marines were different but did not run against the common view. The Navy maintains a forward presence, and at any time many of its vessels are at sea and ready for action. Marine Expeditionary Units are routinely on board Navy surface vessels. The Navy had the highest percentage of personnel with at least one deployment and the highest percentage with at least one hostile deployment. The latter occurred because many vessels were in hos-

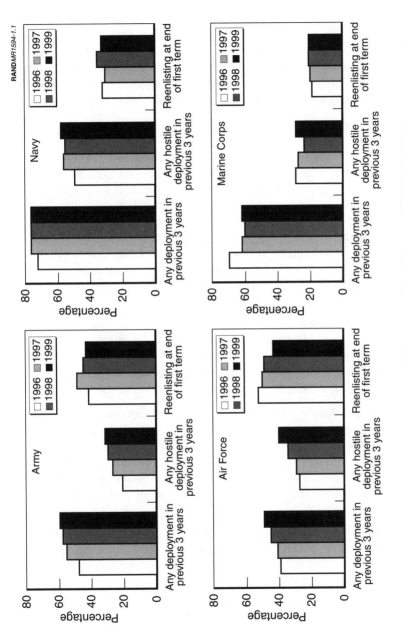

Figure 1.1—Deployment and First-Term Reenlistment, FY1996–FY1999

tile waters for part of their voyage (e.g., patrolling in the Adriatic Sea). The Navy's high percentage of deployment remained stable over FY1996–FY1999, and there was little change in first-term reenlistment. The Marine Corps had a small decline in the percentage of personnel with any deployment or any hostile deployment, and there was hardly any change in Marine first-term reenlistment.

Although Figure 1.1 offers information about the trends in deployment and first-term reenlistment, it is not wise to rely on these patterns for inferences about the effect of deployment on reenlistment. Reenlistment may be affected by other factors, including relative pay, the availability of private-sector jobs, the use of reenlistment bonuses, and non-pecuniary incentives to reenlist, such as stabilization policies that reduce unit turbulence. In addition, the figure may mask differences in the effect of deployment on reenlistment across members. In particular, it does not show whether the number and kind of deployments affected a member's reenlistment decision.

This report addressed three questions relevant to policy:

- **Why might there be a relationship between past deployment and the current decision to reenlist?** In approaching this question, we viewed past deployment as a source of information about the expected utility of future deployment and the probability of future deployment.

- **How did deployment affect the first- and second-term reenlistment decisions of enlisted members?** We estimated reenlistment models for members who faced reenlistment decisions in FY1996–FY1999 and tested whether the effect of deployment was negative or positive, large or small, related to dependency status, and direct as well as possibly indirect, mediated through time to promotion.

- **How would a significant increase in deployment affect reenlistment?** We considered a 25-percent increase in deployments, with all of the increase consisting of deployments with hostile duty.

Our main results came from a one-equation model of the probability of reenlisting as a function of the number and kind of deployments.

This model is in the spirit of the previous research of Hosek and Totten (1998), Wardynski (2000), and Fricker (2002). We also estimated a two-equation model of promotion and reenlistment where deployment affects reenlistment directly and through its influence on the speed of promotion, which in turn affects reenlistment. We studied promotion to paygrade E-5, the first noncommissioned officer rank. This model is a variant of the model introduced by Buddin et al. (1992) and allows the error terms in the promotion and reenlistment equations to be correlated. An error correlation indicates unobserved factors affecting both promotion speed and reenlistment.

We found different relationships for first- and second-term reenlistment, sketched here and described more fully in Chapters Four and Five. The results indicate that deployment was rarely associated with a decrease in reenlistment and often associated with an increase or no change in reenlistment. Among first-term personnel:

- For the Army, Air Force, and Marine Corps, reenlistment increased as nonhostile deployments increased.

- For the Navy, reenlistment was slightly higher for members with some nonhostile deployment compared with members with none, but reenlistment did not rise as nonhostile deployments increased beyond the first.

- For all services, reenlistment changed little as hostile deployments increased.

Among second-term personnel and for all services:

- Reenlistment increased as nonhostile or hostile deployments increased.

- The increase in reenlistment was larger for nonhostile deployments than it was for hostile deployments.

We present a theoretical framework in Chapter Two, where we discuss learning about deployment, expected utility, and the one- and two-equation models of reenlistment used in the empirical work. We discuss the data, the measures of reenlistment, and the measures of deployment and their accuracy in Chapter Three. In Chapter Four, we describe the results of the one-equation model for first- and second-term reenlistment by branch of service. We also discuss the predicted effect on reenlistment of a 25-percent increase in deployments, all hostile. We present the results of the two-equation model of promotion and reenlistment model in Chapter Five and offer our closing thoughts in Chapter Six.

Chapter Two

THEORETICAL FRAMEWORK AND
EMPIRICAL MODELS

This chapter describes our theoretical framework and relates it to the empirical models we use in the data analysis. The theoretical framework provides a means to help explain why past deployment can affect a member's current decision to reenlist. The framework assumes that members have imperfect information about whether they will like or dislike deployment and that they face uncertainty about whether and for how long they will be deployed. The notion of learning from deployments about the frequency, duration, and utility of deployment is therefore a key to understanding why past deployment may affect reenlistment.

We assume that the member is interested in the expected utility of reenlisting for another term. Expected utility depends on deployment, but the features of deployment are not well known to the member. We first describe a mechanism for learning about deployment from actual deployment experience. Then, given the member's estimates of these features, we formulate a model of expected utility. The learning model illustrates how the member can learn from deployment experience, and the expected utility model illustrates how the features of deployment can affect expected utility. The learning and expected utility models are potentially estimable but not with available data. Thus, we rely on the models to clarify our understanding of the relationship between past deployment and reenlistment and to motivate the empirical work.

We describe the two kinds of models we estimate. These are a one-equation model of deployment and reenlistment and a two-equation model of promotion speed and reenlistment, both of which are dependent on deployment. Our working hypothesis is that the enlisted member does not influence the number and duration of deployments, but we discuss the alternative hypotheses that members can self-select deployment or that commanders handpick members for deployment.

LEARNING ABOUT EXPECTED UTILITY OF DEPLOYMENT

We assume that utility may be expressed as $u_d = f(y_d, \delta) + \varepsilon$, where y_d is income inclusive of deployment income, δ is a parameter affecting the level of utility, and ε is a random factor. (We make this function more explicit in the discussion of expected utility, below.) The member does not know the value of δ but knows that δ can take one of two values: $\bar{\delta}$ or $\underline{\delta}$. Utility when deployed is higher at $\delta = \bar{\delta}$ than at $\delta = \underline{\delta}$. The member learns through deployment experience about the probability that $\delta = \bar{\delta}$. The values of $\bar{\delta}$ and $\underline{\delta}$ can vary across members, reflecting heterogeneous tastes.

Deployment experience provides new information that allows beliefs to be updated. The member has a prior belief that the probability of $\delta = \bar{\delta}$ is π_o. The random factor ε has a zero mean and is identically and independently distributed through time with a single-peaked density $h(\varepsilon)$. Under the prior belief, expected utility when deployed is:

$$E u_d = \pi_o f\left(y_d, \bar{\delta}\right) + \left(1 - \pi_o\right) f\left(y_d, \underline{\delta}\right).$$

When a deployment occurs, the member realizes a level of utility $u_d = U_d$, and it is used to revise the prior π_o. Applying Bayes' Theorem, the posterior belief π_1 that $\delta = \bar{\delta}$ given $u_d = U_d$ is:

$$\Pr\left(\delta = \bar{\delta} \mid u_d = U_d\right) = \frac{\Pr\left(u_d = U_d \mid \delta = \bar{\delta}\right)\pi_o}{\Pr\left(u_d = U_d \mid \delta = \bar{\delta}\right)\pi_o + \Pr\left(u_d = U_d \mid \delta = \underline{\delta}\right)\left(1 - \pi_o\right)}$$

$$= \frac{\Pr\left(f\left(y_d, \bar{\delta}\right) + \varepsilon = U_d\right)\pi_o}{\Pr\left(f\left(y_d, \bar{\delta}\right) + \varepsilon = U_d\right)\pi_o + \Pr\left(f\left(y_d, \underline{\delta}\right) + \varepsilon = U_d\right)\left(1 - \pi_o\right)}$$

$$= \frac{h\left(U_d - f\left(y_d, \bar{\delta}\right)\right) \pi_o}{h\left(U_d - f\left(y_d, \bar{\delta}\right)\right) \pi_o + h\left(U_d - f\left(y_d, \underline{\delta}\right)\right)\left(1 - \pi_o\right)}.$$

The expression $h(U_d - f(y_d, \bar{\delta}))$ is the likelihood that the random term takes the particular value $\varepsilon = U_d - f(y_d, \bar{\delta})$ given $\delta = \bar{\delta}$. If, for example, the density $h(\varepsilon)$ is bell-shaped around zero and the value $\varepsilon = U_d - f(y_d, \bar{\delta})$ is approximately equal to zero, then this likelihood is high. By comparison, $h(U_d - f(y_d, \underline{\delta}))$ is the likelihood that the random term takes the particular value $\varepsilon = U_d - f(y_d, \underline{\delta})$ given $\delta = \underline{\delta}$. If, as mentioned, $\varepsilon = U_d - f(y_d, \bar{\delta})$ is approximately equal to zero and therefore has a high likelihood, then $\varepsilon = U_d - f(y_d, \underline{\delta})$ is likely to be farther from zero and have a lower likelihood. The higher likelihood of $\varepsilon = U_d - f(y_d, \bar{\delta})$ versus $\varepsilon = U_d - f(y_d, \underline{\delta})$ means that $\bar{\delta}$ fits the realized utility U_d better than $\underline{\delta}$. As a result, the posterior belief that $\delta = \bar{\delta}$ is higher than the prior belief—that is, π_1 is greater than π_o.[1]

An increase in the probability that deployment is a high-utility experience increases the expected value of δ and therefore expected utility. Because the likelihood of reenlistment depends on expected utility, the likelihood of reenlistment also increases. Furthermore, multiple deployments provide multiple opportunities to revise beliefs about deployment. If each deployment proved to be a positive experience, for example, the probability of reenlistment would rise with the number of deployments.[2] Similarly, the member can update his or her belief about the probability and duration of deployment.

The same framework can be applied to different types of deployment, such as those that involve hostile duty. Hostile deployments have higher danger, which could mean that $\bar{\delta}$ and $\underline{\delta}$ are both lower than they are for nonhostile deployments. By treating hostile and

---

[1]The analysis can be extended to allow the parameter to take a continuum of values, but this does not add insight.

[2]We identified the separation from family and friends as a generic aspect of deployment. The utility loss from this separation might change as deployments increase. For instance, a military spouse or close friend might get used to handling things on his or her own and become less distressed with each deployment.

nonhostile deployments separately, we allow the data to determine whether they have different relationships to reenlistment.

EXPECTED UTILITY

The member's willingness to reenlist depends in part on deployment, but future deployment is uncertain. Given this uncertainty, the member considers the expected utility of reenlisting. We assume that the member has subjective estimates of the frequency and duration of deployment, knows about deployment-related pays, and has a sense of the fixed and variable costs of deployment, e.g., arranging to have someone look after personal belongings and perhaps the cost of additional child care as the spouse copes with the member's absence. The member has preferences over the amount of time deployed versus time at home station, the variance of the number of deployments, and the variance of the duration of deployment.

We develop an expression for the expected utility of the term. We show that the expected utility can increase and then decrease as the expected deployments increase. Also, it can be positively or negatively related to the expected length of a deployment.[3] As mentioned, the connection between the expected utility of the term and the learning model is that, through past experience, the member learns about his or her preferences for deployment and about the mean and variance of deployments and deployment duration. The expected utility model provides a framework to put this learning to use.

Number of Deployments

The number of deployments during a three- to four-year term can be reasonably well described by a Poisson distribution. Given the actual

---

[3]The derivation of expected utility is conditional on the member's subjective estimates of the variance of deployments and deployment length and those preferences regarding time deployed and the variances of deployments and deployment length. We could extend the derivation of expected utility to take the expectation over these estimates by using the posterior distribution of their values, but no further insight would be gained.

distribution of deployments, we assume there are four possible outcomes: zero, one, two, or three deployments. The probability of four or more deployments is small enough to be negligible. We can see this by considering several Poisson distributions that reflect the observed distribution of deployments. The Poisson distribution has a single parameter, λ. For a given λ, the probability of n deployments ($n = 0, 1, 2, \ldots$) is $e^{-\lambda}\lambda^n/n!$. The mean and variance equal λ, and the probability of having one or more deployments rises with λ. Table 2.1 shows the probability of n deployments for values of λ that approximately correspond to the Army and Air Force ($\lambda = 0.5$) and to the Navy and Marine Corps ($\lambda = 1.1$).

Length of Deployment

We approximate the distribution of deployment length by a continuous distribution defined over the range of zero to 2μ. The mean duration is μ and the variance of duration is $\mu^2/3$. This is not as good an approximation as the Poisson is for the number of deployments, but it is good enough for our purpose of showing how learning can be applied to the expected utility calculation. The probability of a deployment of length s equals $1/(2\mu)$. We assume deployment lengths are independent of the number of deployments and also independent of each other. Therefore, the probability of n deployments of lengths $s_1, s_2, s_3, \ldots, s_n$ is $(e^{-\lambda}\lambda^n/n!)(1/(2\mu)^n)$. The total time deployed is $d(n, s_1, s_2, s_3, \ldots, s_n) = \sum_{i=1}^{n} s_i$.

Table 2.1

Deployment Frequency Based on Poisson Distribution

Deployments	$\lambda = 0.5$	$\lambda = 1.1$
0	0.61	0.33
1	0.30	0.37
2	0.08	0.20
3	0.01	0.07
4	0.002	0.02
5	0.0002	0.004

Deployment-Related Pay and Cost

The member receives a base income of m_o dollars for the term. When deployed, the member receives deployment pay of w' dollars per unit time and incurs a cost of c dollars per unit time, for a net deployment pay rate of $w = w' - c$. The member incurs a fixed cost k for each deployment. Total income is $m = m_o + wd - nk$. (We comment further on net deployment pay below.)

Utility Function

We assume utility depends on purchased goods x, time not deployed h, time deployed d, the variance of deployments λ, and the variance of deployment length, which is proportional to μ^2. For the Poisson and Uniform distributions, which have one parameter, a higher variance implies a higher mean. The parameters λ and μ are dictated by the needs of the service, although the member must estimate their values.

If the member were free to choose time deployed as well as purchased goods, he or she would select the values that maximize utility:

$$Max\, L = U(x, T - d, d) + \varphi(m_0 + wd - nk - x).$$

This leads to the first-order conditions:

$$U_x = \varphi,$$
$$U_{T-d} = U_d + \varphi w,$$
$$m_0 + wd - nk - x = 0.$$

The first condition states that the marginal utility of purchased goods equals the marginal utility of income (φ) multiplied by the price of purchased goods, which is assumed to equal one. In the second condition, the marginal utility of time at home station $(T - d)$ is equated to the marginal utility of time deployed (d) plus the marginal utility of the net deployment-related pay. If net deployment pay is zero, the member would prefer an amount of time deployed such that its marginal utility equaled the marginal utility of time at home station. If net deployment pay is positive, the member prefers more time deployed. Even though additional time deployed can be assumed to have a lower marginal utility, the additional pay offsets the decrease in marginal utility. The third condition states that the member exhausts the budget constraint.

The first-order conditions implicitly define the member's demands for purchased goods and time deployed as functions of base income, net deployment pay, fixed cost of deployment, price of purchased goods (which we set equal to 1), and parameters of the utility function. We can use the indirect utility function to describe how utility is affected when the member cannot choose the time deployed but must accept what the service assigns. The member's utility is highest if the assigned time deployed equals the amount the member would have chosen according to the first-order conditions. Higher or lower levels of time deployed reduce utility relative to that optimum.

Because members have chosen to be in military service, it is reasonable to focus on interior solutions where the preferred time deployed is positive but does not use all available time. Moreover, because time deployed trades off against time not deployed, utility rises as time deployed increases from zero to its optimal value, and then declines as time deployed crowds out time at home station. We use a quadratic function to approximate this relationship.

As shown above, the number and duration of deployments depend on the distribution parameters λ and μ. The member's income and total time deployed depend on the number and length of deployments. Therefore, one possibility is to write utility, given the occurrence of n deployments of lengths $s_1, s_2, s_3, ..., s_n$, as

$$U(m, n, s_1, s_2, s_3, ..., s_n) = \log m + ad - bd^2 - c\lambda - f\mu^2.$$

Utility increases with a and decreases with b ($a, b > 0$). If there were no deployment pay or cost so income did not depend on deployment, the optimal amount of time deployed would be $a/2b$. The member's expected utility, developed below, is a weighted sum of the probability of the outcome of n deployments of given lengths multiplied by the utility of that outcome. Because the utility of any outcome with positive deployment ($n > 0$) is positively related to a and negatively related to b, it follows that expected utility is also positively related to a and negatively related to b. The learning model described how the member learned about his or her preferences for deployment (i.e., about the values of a, b, c, and f in the utility function) and about the mean and variance of the number and duration of deployment (i.e., about λ and μ).

Expected Utility Function

We form the expected utility function from its parts:

- The expected utility, given zero deployments:

$$EU_0 = m_0 - c\lambda - f\mu^2.$$

- The expected utility, given one deployment:

$$EU_1 = \int_0^{2\mu} (\log(m_0 + ws - k) + as - bs^2c\lambda - f\mu^2)\frac{1}{2\mu}ds.$$

- The expected utility, given two deployments:

$$EU_2 = \int_0^{2\mu}\int_0^{2\mu} (\log(m_0 + w(s_1 + s_2) - 2k) + a(s_1 + s_2)$$
$$- b(s_1 + s_2)^2 - c\lambda - f\mu^2)\frac{1}{(2\mu)^2}ds_1 ds_2.$$

- The expected utility, given three deployments:

$$EU_3 = \int_0^{2\mu}\int_0^{2\mu}\int_0^{2\mu} (\log(m_0 + w(s_1 + s_2 + s_3) - 3k) + a(s_1 + s_2 + s_3)$$
$$- b(s_1 + s_2 + s_3)^2 - c\lambda - f\mu^2)\frac{1}{(2\mu)^3}ds_1 ds_2 ds_3.$$

Keeping the foregoing expressions in mind, the expected utility can be written compactly as:

$$EU = e^\lambda EU_0 + e^\lambda \lambda EU_1 + \frac{e^\lambda \lambda^2}{2}EU_2 + \frac{e^\lambda \lambda^3}{6}EU_3.$$

When the integrals for EU1, EU2, and EU3 are evaluated, we obtain an explicit form for expected utility. We have completed the integration and can use the explicit form to show how expected utility varies with its parameters: a, b, c, f, λ, and μ^2.[4]

This expected utility function is flexible enough to capture a variety of relationships between deployment and expected utility. We have already mentioned that expected utility increases with a and decreases with b, and that apart from net deployment pay, the member's preferred time deployed is $a/2b$. Because sailors join the Navy knowing they can expect a rotation of six months at sea and twelve months at home port, they probably have a higher value of a relative to b than do soldiers or airmen, who may not expect or prefer to be away as much. With respect to the learning model, we have argued that incoming members hold naive preferences about time deployed. Members learn more about deployment by being deployed, and, based on their experience, they may revise the prior values of their preferences. For instance, if a is revised upward because of a deployment, the level of expected utility rises and the member is more likely to reenlist. If a is revised upward with each deployment, the probability of reenlistment should rise with the number of deployments. This is not a necessary relationship, but it is a possibility that can be readily handled within the learning model and the expected utility model. Because our empirical work often shows an increase in reenlistment with the number of deployments, this is a relevant possibility to keep in mind.

We can also show that for reasonable parameters, expected utility is likely to increase with λ, up to a point, even though it has a negative direct effect on utility. (Again, λ equals the variance and the mean of the number of deployments.) Expected utility increases because an increase in λ increases expected time deployed, which initially has a high marginal utility.

Furthermore, we can show the relationship between expected utility and the variance of deployment duration. It seems reasonable that, controlling for the number of deployments, members with more actual time deployed are likely to revise upward their estimated mean and variance of deployment duration. (Again, the mean duration is μ and the variance of duration is $\mu^2/3$.) The theoretical

---

[4]The results of the integration are available from the authors on request.

model shows that a higher variance (or mean) can lead to either an increase or decrease in expected utility, depending on parameter values. In our empirical work, we find that time deployed has a positive effect on reenlistment for first-term Army members and a negative effect on reenlistment for first-term members in the other services. Yet, these seemingly contradictory effects are not inconsistent with the expected utility model.

We use two sets of parameter values to illustrate these points. Parameter set 1 has $75,000 base income during the term, net deployment pay of $75 per month, and a fixed cost of $200 per deployment. The member prefers about 7.5 months deployed ($a = 0.15$, $b = 0.01$) and is indifferent to the variances of deployments and deployment duration ($c = 0, f = 0$). Parameter set 2 has a base income of $75,000, net deployment pay of $200 per month, a fixed cost of $200 per deployment, a preference for about 15 months deployed ($a = 0.30$, $b = 0.01$), and an aversion to variance in the number and duration of deployment ($c = 0.02, f = 0.04$). Parameter set 1 roughly corresponds to a preference for time deployed that we might expect among soldiers and airmen, whereas parameter set 2 seems more descriptive of sailors and marines.

Figure 2.1 shows the relationship between expected utility and the variance of the number of deployments (λ) for parameter sets 1 and 2.[5] We show the relationship at several different values of the variance of deployment duration ($v \equiv \mu^2/3$). The similarity in the curves implies that the relationship is not sensitive to duration variance. With parameter set 1, expected utility rises with λ over the range of λ that seems relevant to soldiers and airmen. That is, from Table 2.1 we know that when $\lambda = 0.5$, about 40 percent of members have one or more deployments, and three-fourths of those members have a single deployment. Thus, in this range, learning that led a member to increase the subjective value of λ would be associated with higher expected utility, hence a higher probability of reenlistment.

---

[5]The left- and right-hand panels in Figure 2.1 use different scales. Because utility functions are unique only up to a monotone transformation, the scale is arbitrary. The main purpose of the figure is to show how expected utility varies with the variance of deployments. Similar comments apply to Figure 2.2, which shows expected utility with respect to the variance of deployment length.

RAND*MR1594-2.1*

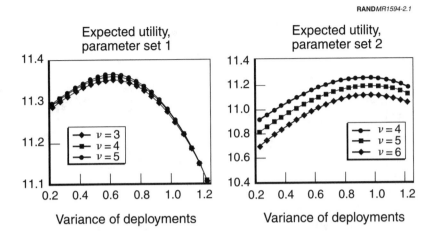

Figure 2.1—Relationship Between Expected Utility and the Variance of Deployments for Parameter Sets 1 and 2

With parameter set 2, expected utility is relatively flat in the range from $\lambda = 0.85$ to $\lambda = 1.05$, a range consistent with the number and variance of deployments sailors and marines might have expected when they signed up. However, for lower values of λ, expected utility declines. This suggests that if deployment was much lower than initially expected and preferred, λ would be revised down and expected utility would be reduced. A high amount of deployment, leading to a large upward revision of λ, would also be associated with lower expected utility.

Figure 2.2 shows the relationship between expected utility and the variance of deployment duration for each parameter set. With parameter set 1, expected utility rises with duration variance because the increase in variance implies an increase in mean duration; for these parameter values, expected utility rises with duration. With parameter set 2, expected utility declines with duration variance. In this case, a decline occurs because of the negative effect of the variance on expected utility, and also because the rise in variance implies an increase in mean duration, which leads to more time deployed than the member prefers.

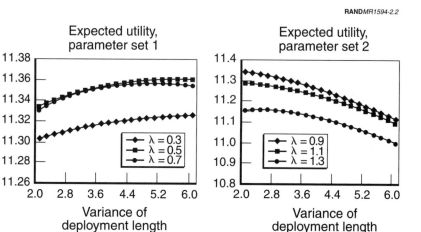

Figure 2.2—Relationship Between Expected Utility and the Variance of
Deployment Duration for Parameter Sets 1 and 2

Net Deployment Pay

Because utility when deployed depends on net deployment pay,
policy can affect utility by the use of deployment pays and by steps to
reduce a member's fixed and variable cost of deployment.

Deployment pays—such as Family Separation Allowance (FSA),
Hostile Fire/Imminent Danger Pay (referred to in this report as HFP),
Combat Zone Tax Exclusion, Career Sea Pay, and (as of February
1999) Hardship Duty Pay—compensate for separation from dependents, unusual danger, arduous duty, and inhospitable circumstances. By increasing income during deployment, deployment pays
reduce the extent to which these adverse aspects of deployment
decrease a member's utility. Because deployment pays are set by
policy, they should tend to be higher for more-demanding or riskier
deployments. Because they are set ahead of time, they may not be
well targeted for a particular deployment; however, it is easy for a
member to factor them into expected utility.[6]

---

[6]We could not estimate the effect of deployment pays on reenlistment because their
levels changed little in our data period.

In addition to compensating for the adverse aspects of deployment, deployment pays help offset a member's fixed and variable costs of deployment. A junior enlisted member with no dependents may have a low cost of deployment. However, if the member owns a car, has bills to pay (e.g., loan payments, telephone bills), or lives off base and has belongings to take care of (e.g., TV, disc player, dog), then arrangements must be made. These arrangements represent a fixed cost for each deployment, while handling the arrangements when deployed is a variable cost that continues for the duration of deployment. Married members can rely on their spouse to handle personal affairs, which suggests that the fixed and variable cost may be shifted to the spouse. The spouse may have to adjust his or her schedule in response to the member's absence (e.g., work fewer hours or less convenient hours; buy, rather than cook, more meals; use more baby-sitting; perform more home maintenance).

On base, family support services are available to help military spouses cope with the stress of separation and the added responsibility of running a household when the member is deployed. These services may be thought of as in-kind deployment pays. Family support services can, for example, put a military spouse in touch with counselors and provide suggestions regarding child-care providers. Family support groups create telephone trees to relay messages about the deployed unit members to their spouses and friends. Also, the services provide such communication links as e-mail and weekly telephone calls so that deployed members can stay in touch.

It follows from Bayesian updating that the net deployment pay affects the posterior belief π_1 that $\delta = \bar{\delta}$. For a given realized utility U_d, as net income increases, the value of π_1 *decreases*. This occurs because utility depends on net pay and the value of δ, and the same level of utility can be produced by a low income and high δ ($\delta = \bar{\delta}$) or a high income and low δ ($\delta = \underline{\delta}$). Therefore, for a given realized utility, the probability that $\delta = \bar{\delta}$ is lower when the level of income is higher.

Deployment and Promotion Speed

Deployment might also affect reenlistment through promotion speed. Because income, responsibility, and authority increase with rank, we assume that reaching the next rank faster increases expected utility and reenlistment. The expected utility model can be extended into a dynamic programming model of retention, but we do not make that transformation here.[7]

Deployment could affect promotion speed in several ways. Deployment could increase or decrease the amount of time available for reading and studying for promotion. It could also affect the member's willingness to exert effort toward promotion. A member might infer that future utility when deployed is higher at a higher rank. Also, the services may value deployment experience in making promotions to the extent that it results in decorations, awards, improved physical condition, greater skill and knowledge, or a higher rating of future potential.[8]

As with reenlistment, the relationship between deployment and promotion speed is an empirical matter. The effect may differ between nonhostile and hostile episodes of deployment. Hostile deployment may provide less off-duty time for the member and be more physically demanding, making it harder to prepare for promotion. However, hostile deployment might be more likely to be recognized by a decoration or award.

Summary

We have presented a learning mechanism that describes how a member might revise his or her prior beliefs about deployment and a model of expected utility that describes how a member can utilize that knowledge when deciding whether to reenlist. In particular, the member may learn about preferences for time deployed relative to time not deployed, preferences for the variance of deployments and the variance of deployment duration, and the variances (and means) themselves. We also showed how deployment pays and the fixed and variable costs of deployment enter into expected utility.

---

[7]Hosek and Totten (1998) put deployment, promotion, and reenlistment in the context of a dynamic programming model, building on the work of Gotz and McCall (1984) and Asch and Warner (1994).

[8]Williamson (1999) describes the services' enlisted promotion systems; every service takes into account the factors we mention above.

The learning and expected utility models provide a conceptual framework for connecting past deployments to a member's current reenlistment decision. The learning model allows prior beliefs to be revised up or down, and therefore does not imply any particular relationship between deployment and posterior beliefs. The expected utility model, as it has been specified, allows for a number of relationships that helped to motivate our empirical work and aided in interpreting the results:

- The expected utility model implies that an upward revision in the preferred time deployed (i.e., an upward revision in a and a downward revision in b) causes an increase in expected utility, hence in the probability of reenlistment. Therefore, if deployment typically led to an upward revision, that would be reflected by higher reenlistment.

- Depending on parameter values, an increase in the mean or variance of deployment may increase or decrease expected utility. The relationship between expected utility and the mean or variance of deployment is an inverted u-shape. For parameter values that seem relevant to members of the Army and Air Force, an increase in the mean or variance of deployment leads to an increase in expected utility. For parameter values that seem relevant to the Navy and Marine Corps, an increase in the mean or variance of deployment has little effect on expected utility. However, a sizeable reduction in the mean or variance of deployment is likely to reduce expected utility. A sizeable reduction might occur if, for example, a member entered the Navy or Marine Corps expecting a high rate of deployment by going to sea, but actually had no deployment.

- Depending on parameter values, an increase in the mean or variance of the length of a deployment might increase or decrease expected utility. Controlling for the number of deployments, more time deployed might cause an upward revision in the value of the mean or variance of deployment length. Because this could either increase or decrease expected utility, it is possible to observe a positive or a negative effect of time deployed on the probability of reenlistment.

- Expected utility is positively related to income. Income is higher with higher base pay and higher with rate of deployment pay but is lower with higher fixed and variable cost of deployment. These relationships are potentially testable, but during our study period deployment pays were nearly constant. Also, we have no data on a member's cost of deployment. Therefore, the effect of deployment pay and cost is not observed directly but intertwined with the variables indicating deployment.

- Deployment might affect reenlistment by speeding up, or slowing down, the time to promotion. Faster promotion leads to higher pay, and service at a higher rank, with its greater authority and responsibility, might be more satisfying. Perhaps deployment is more satisfying when experienced at a higher rank; perhaps not. If deployment speeds up promotion, we would expect an increase in reenlistment.

- The preference for deployment may depend on the characteristics of deployment. For instance, deployment involving hostile duty might have as many or more positive aspects than deployment that does not involve hostile duty, but hostile deployment probably has more negative aspects (high stress, poor conditions, long hours, disease, combat risks).

EMPIRICAL MODELS

Our basic model of deployment and reenlistment is a probit regression. Let y_i be the member's propensity to reenlist and x_i represent the explanatory variables. In the probit model:

$$y_i = \beta x_i + v_i$$
$$v_i \sim N(0,1)$$
$$\Pr(reenlist) = \Pr(y_i > 0)$$
$$= \Pr(\beta x_i + v_i > 0)$$
$$= \Phi(\beta x_i)$$
$$\Pr(not\ reenlist) = 1 - \Phi(\beta x_i).$$

The error term v_i represents unobserved factors that influence the reenlistment decision. The error term is normally distributed with zero mean and unit variance, and $\Phi(\cdot)$ is the standardized normal distribution. In the data, each member's reenlistment decision and explanatory variables are observed. A likelihood function is created by multiplying together the probabilities of reenlistment for those who reenlist, and the probabilities of non-reenlistment for those who do not. The likelihood function is maximized with respect to the parameters β to obtain estimates of the parameters and their standard deviations.

The explanatory variables include indicator variables for the number and kind (hostile/nonhostile) of deployments over a three-year period ending three months prior to the date at which the member made a decision to reenlist or leave. There are indicator variables for one, two, or three or more nonhostile deployments, and one, two, or three or more hostile deployments. We also define interactions among the deployment indicator variables, and in exploratory specifications we enter the total months deployed in addition to the deployment indicators. Other explanatory variables include the member's Armed Forces Qualification Test (AFQT) category, education, occupational area, race/ethnicity, gender, dependency status, fiscal year in which the member's current term ends or a reenlistment decision is made, the unemployment rate at the start of the current term, and the current unemployment rate.

Our promotion/reenlistment model allows deployment to affect reenlistment directly and indirectly through its effect on promotion speed. Promotion speed is measured by t_i, the number of months to E-5 (the first noncommissioned officer rank).[9] The structure of the model is as follows:

$$t_i = \alpha z_i + \eta_i$$
$$y_i = \beta x_i + \gamma t_i + v_i$$
$$\begin{pmatrix} \eta_i \\ v_i \end{pmatrix} \sim N\left(\begin{pmatrix} 0 \\ 0 \end{pmatrix}, \begin{pmatrix} \sigma^2 & \rho \\ \rho & 1 \end{pmatrix} \right).$$

Here, γ is an estimate of the effect of promotion time on reenlistment. If a longer time to promotion indicates a poorer fit with the military, we expect γ to be negative. The model allows for the pos-

---

[9]Unlike the other services, Navy promotions occur on a six-month cycle. Therefore, the time unit in the Navy is six months rather than one month.

sibility that unobserved factors affect promotion speed and reenlistment. Such factors may reflect the member's effort, ability, and
commitment to military service. After controlling for the observed
variables, if a shorter time to promotion is associated with a higher
probability of reenlistment, the error correlation ρ will be negative.

Model estimation is complicated because many observations on
promotion time are censored. Censoring arises when a member has
not been promoted before leaving service or before the end of the
data window. If t_i^c is the censoring date, the probability that promotion occurs after that date is:

$$\Pr(t_i \text{ less than } t_i^c) = \Pr(\alpha z_i + \eta_i > t_i^c)$$
$$= \Pr(\eta_i > t_i^c - \alpha z_i)$$
$$= 1 - \Phi(t_i^c - \alpha z_i).$$

Because promotion time and reenlistment are assumed to follow a
bivariate normal distribution, the model uses an expression for the
joint probability of, say, reenlistment and censored time to promotion.[10] If a member does not reenlist, the promotion process is followed up to the time of departure. If a member reenlists, the promotion process is followed up to the time of promotion or the end of
the data window.

To identify the effect of expected time to E-5 on reenlistment, the
promotion equation includes some variables that are not in the
reenlistment equation. These are indicators of whether the member
was fast to the previous pay grade, E-4, and the quarter of the year in
which the member entered service. The speed to E-4 is specified by
indicators of whether the member's time to E-4 was in the 25th, 50th,
or 75th percentile relative to those in his or her entry cohort who

---

[10]The probability of reenlistment and censored time to promotion is

$$\int_{-\beta x}^{\infty} \int_{t^c - \alpha z}^{\infty} \phi(0, \Sigma) d\eta \, du,$$

where ϕ is the normal density and Σ is the covariance matrix.

reached E-4.[11]   Otherwise, the variables in the promotion equation include AFQT, education, occupational area, and fiscal year.

WHAT IF DEPLOYMENT IS SELECTIVE?

We think the assumption that deployment is exogenous to the member is appropriate for our empirical analysis of first- and second-term reenlistment. Junior enlisted members typically have little say in choosing their assignments and missions. However, Wardynski (2000) raised the possibility that a member or the member's commanding officer can affect whether the member deploys.

If a member influences deployment, the influence will be directed toward increasing the level of expected utility. Members who want more deployment will seek to increase their deployment, while those who prefer less deployment will seek the opposite. Therefore, if members can self-select, the probability of reenlistment should increase for those who want more deployment and those who do not. It is unknown whether the difference between their reenlistment probabilities would widen or narrow. We note this because the empirical analysis contrasts the reenlistment probability of deployers to nondeployers. Self-selection would not necessarily make deployers appear more likely to reenlist than nondeployers and therefore would not necessarily bias upward the effect of deployment on reenlistment.

The commanding officer presumably seeks to exclude from deployment those members with poor attitudes or poor performance. The commander's scope for culling the ranks depends on whether replacements can be found, if needed, to keep unit manning at the level required for the deployment. Some excluded members might have preferred not to deploy, so exclusion would increase their expected utility. Other excluded members might have preferred to deploy, so exclusion would reduce their expected income. If the commanding officer removed members with poor attitudes or poor performance who were unlikely to reenlist, the average reenlistment probability would increase among members who deploy and decrease among members who do not deploy. This may increase or

---

[11]We also estimated the model without the E-4 indicators, as discussed below.

reduce the estimated effect of deployment on the reenlistment probability. If the reenlistment probability of deployers is initially higher
than that of nondeployers, then commander-selection increases this
positive difference. If the reenlistment probability of deployers is
initially lower than that of nondeployers, then commander-selection
reduces this negative difference and possibly creates a positive difference. Thus, commander-selection may exaggerate or reduce the
estimated effect of deployment on the reenlistment probability,
depending on the initial values.

Anticipating the empirical results, we found that reenlistment tended
to increase with nonhostile episodes of deployment. It is possible
that commander selection biased upward an already-positive relationship between deployment and reenlistment. We also found that
reenlistment was little affected by hostile deployments. If the true
effect of hostile episodes on reenlistment were negative, commander
selection might have changed the negative effect to a zero effect.

We should also ask whether commander selection of those who
deploy affects our ability to identify the effect of expected time to E-5
promotion on reenlistment. This effect is identified by the two variables in the promotion equation that are not in the reenlistment
equation, namely, time to E-4 and quarter of accession. Members
with short times to E-4 promotion (controlling for AFQT, education,
and occupational area) are high performers and may have high tastes
for the military. If so, the expected time to E-5, which depends on
time to E-4 and presumably, taste, might be correlated with the error
term in the reenlistment equation. This could bias its coefficients. If
a longer expected time to E-5 reduced reenlistment, the bias would
probably make this negative relationship steeper.

Although these are possibilities, we have no firm evidence on the role
played by commander selection or self-selection. If the role is minor
and perhaps negligible, as we suspect, there should be little effect on
our estimates.

Chapter Three

DATA AND MEASURES OF DEPLOYMENT

This section describes our data and the definitions of reenlistment and deployment. The reenlistment indicator is based on stay/leave behavior drawn from the services' personnel records, and the measures of deployment are derived from indicators of the receipt of FSA and HFP. The measures appear to be a reliable basis for analyzing the relationship between reenlistment and long or hostile deployment. Such deployments are typical of peacetime military operations, such as peacemaking and peacekeeping. They also include deployments for war, although there was no war in our data period. As discussed below and documented in Appendix B, the number of deployments measured in the data may undercount the true number of deployments, but the undercount is quite small. Although our empirical analysis focuses on deployments, we also developed measures of total months of deployment. The measure probably undercounts months on the order of one to two weeks per deployment, that is, by a modest amount.

DATA

We use the Proxy PERSTEMPO data file, which was created by the Defense Manpower Data Center (DMDC). Our file contains longitudinal data on active-duty personnel by month from January 1993 through September 1999 and for the last month in each quarter going back to FY1988. For enlisted members, the file has obligated service, education, occupational area, AFQT category, demographics, dependency status, and indicators of deployment based on the receipt of two deployment-related pays: FSA and HFP.

REENLISTMENT DEFINED

For many members, the decision to reenlist or leave occurs on or before the end of their term of service. Some members extend their term of service and push their reenlist/leave decision forward. We handle extenders by following them to the point where they make their reenlist/leave decision.

First-Term Reenlistment

New recruits enter service under a contract that stipulates the length of their term of service, which ranges from two to six years and is most commonly four years. The expiration of term of service (ETS) date for the end of the *first* term of service is given on the personnel data file.[1]

First-term members may take one of three actions on or before the ETS date for the end of their term. They may reenlist, extend, or leave. Reenlistment and extension both increase the service obligation, but the data do not indicate whether the increase is an extension or a reenlistment. We use the convention that an increase in ETS date of 24 months or more is a reenlistment, while an increase of 1 to 23 months is an extension. Members who extend usually extend only once and often for less than 12 months. Because our focus is on reenlistment, we track personnel who extend until they reenlist or leave. Normally, members who leave do so at their ETS date, but in some cases the service may permit an early-out.

A member's decision to reenlist, extend, or leave can be affected by military pay, civilian pay, unemployment rate, reenlistment bonus, and special options, such as the choice of location or opportunity to retrain. These factors are not available on the PERSTEMPO file and typically change from year to year. We use fiscal year indicators to control for the combined influence of civilian pay, military pay, and total bonus budgets, which change each year. The indicators offer some control for the unemployment rate, which has within- and between-year change. But the indicators do not control for specialty-

---

[1]To be more specific, the file indicates the number of months left until the ETS date for the first term.

specific variation in bonuses, training availability, or choice of location.

With the above in mind, we constructed an analytical database by identifying when a member faced a reenlistment decision. For first-term members, this was the fiscal year containing the ETS date of their first term, the fiscal year of a reenlistment decision if it was made early, or, if they have extended, the ETS date based on the extension. The data covered ETS dates in FY1996–FY1999. We started at FY1996 because we defined our deployment variables over a three-year window preceding the reenlistment decision and needed monthly data, which went back only to January 1993, to do so. We ended with FY1999 because it was the last year of our data.

For each first-term member with an ETS date in a given fiscal year, we followed the member's record to observe changes in the ETS date. If the date did not change and the member left on or before the ETS date, he or she was recorded as a leaver as of the date of leaving. If the date increased by 24 or more months on or before the ETS date, the member was recorded as a reenlistee as of the date the increase occurred. The additional obligation of service was added to the end of the existing obligation, even if the reenlistment decision was made early. If the ETS date increased by 1 to 23 months, we classified the member as having extended and followed him or her to the decision to reenlist or leave. The months of extension were added to the end of the existing obligation. If the new ETS date fell in a future fiscal year, the member was carried over to that year and processed as above.

Extensions may be made for a number of reasons. For example, a member may extend to obtain training required before being allowed to reenlist in a different specialty. A member may extend for reasons of personal convenience, such as staying in a location until a son or daughter finishes the school year or until the member's spouse finishes a project at work. A member may extend to have enough time remaining in service for eligibility to deploy for a particular posting or mission. Because an extension might be made in conjunction with a deployment, a member might have some influence over his or her deployment experience. We did not have data on how often this occurred, but we believe it is infrequent.

Second-Term Reenlistment

Having identified the first-term reenlistment decision date, we could identify a new ETS date *given first-term reenlistment.* As in the first term, we used the date to place a member in a fiscal year, then followed the member to detect departure, reenlistment, or extension, and if the latter, when reenlistment or departure eventually occurred.

DEPLOYMENT MEASURES

Deployment Measures Defined

We constructed two measures from the PERSTEMPO file: deployments and months of deployment. Both measures involve counts over a three-year window ending three months before the month of the reenlist or leave decision. The three-month "buffer" was intended to control for possible reverse causality. If a member was near the end of the term, learned that the unit would be deployed, and wanted to go on the deployment, then that specific deployment could influence the member's decision to reenlist. But that deployment, falling in the three-month window, was not included in our count.

To implement a count over a three-year window, we needed members who had at least three and a half years of service at the time of their reenlistment decision. Members with two- and three-year terms were therefore excluded from our analysis sample unless they had extended the length of their term. Two-year terms were offered in the Army's 2+2+4 option, which required two years of active duty, two years of selected reserve duty, and four years of Individual Ready Reserve to complete the eight-year service obligation. The Army, Navy, and Marine Corps offered three-year terms. Four-year terms are relatively more common, and bonuses induce some members to select longer terms over three-year terms. Because bonuses influence the choice of term length, a longer term does not necessarily reflect a higher taste for military service.

We built similar measures of deployment for promotion. We specified a three-year window prior to a member's E-5 promotion date or

RAND*MR1594-3.1*

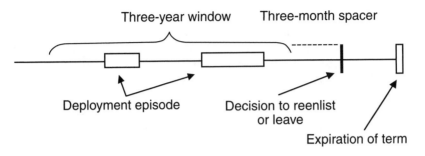

Figure 3.1—Counting Deployments

censoring date, which was the end of the first term if the member did not reach E-5 and separated, or was the end of our data window (September 1999). Figure 3.1 illustrates the window for counting episodes and months of deployment.

We derived deployment measures from the receipt of FSA or HFP, or both. FSA is payable to members with dependents who are away on duty for a period of at least 30 consecutive days. (Dependents include spouses and children.) A small percentage of members with dependents do not have a spouse. HFP is payable to members on duty in areas or circumstances deemed hostile. (Appendix A describes the pays more fully.) HFP is payable regardless of whether a member has dependents.

For members with dependents, a deployment consists of a string of months in which FSA or HFP, or both, are received. The three-year window includes complete deployments as well as those that ended or began in the window.

FSA is not payable to members without dependents and so cannot be used to infer their nonhostile deployments. When a member has no dependents, we impute nonhostile deployment from a DMDC-constructed indicator of unit deployment. A deployment consists of a string of months in which a unit-deployment indicator is imputed, HFP is received, or both. The unit deployment indicator represents the condition where a unit consists of at least 10 members, at least 30 percent of the members have dependents, and at least 60 percent of the members with dependents receive FSA or HFP, or both.

The total of months deployed *in the three-year period* is the sum of months for each deployment in the period. Some deployments start before or end after the three-year period, so total months deployed in the three-year period is less than the count of months of all completed deployments that have at least one month in the three-year window. However, we computed the mean and variance of months per deployment by using the subset of deployments completed within the three-year window.

Many members marry while in service, so it is common for dependency status to change. About 15 percent of enlisted members are married at entry, 40 percent by the end of the first term, and 75 percent by the end of the second term. The deployment counts of many personnel are hybrids of deployment as measured in the months without dependents and in the months with dependents.

Critique of Deployment Measures

The deployment measures are based on pays, FSA and HFP, and are therefore likely to be a comprehensive and reliable record of deployments relative to self-reports, periodic surveys, or even personnel records. The circumstances that trigger payment of FSA or HFP account for an important subset of deployments. These include peacemaking, peacekeeping, lengthy humanitarian or disaster relief missions, deployments involving high risk, and tours that involve lengthy separation from dependents. The presence of HFP enables deployments to be designated as hostile or nonhostile, where hostile means that HFP was received in *any* month of an episode.

However, the deployment measures may under- or overcount deployments and months of deployment. We believe the count of deployments is accurate,[2] but there appears to be an undercount of

---

[2]The use of FSA to count nonhostile episodes is accurate for episodes of at least 30 days. Shorter nonhostile episodes are not eligible for FSA and therefore are not captured by our count. The "days away" measure of deployment recently developed by the DMDC captures short nonhostile deployments. The "days away" measure does not identify the purpose of the days away (e.g., whether for training, for a mission, for

months. We calculate that the undercount is small (see Appendix B). FSA and HFP measures of deployment miss such short, nonhostile temporary duty as some major-command exercises, joint exercises, schooling, training, and travel that is related to routine operations, maintenance, acquisition, logistic, medical, and personnel activities. The deployment measures contain no information on the purpose, location, conditions, and risks of the deployment.

SUMMARY

We use two deployment-related pays, FSA and HFP, to create variables for deployments, months of deployment, and whether a deployment involved hostile duty. The measures refer to a three-year period ending three months before the member's reenlist or leave decision. The deployments include all missions with hostile duty, regardless of their length, and all missions or assignments with at least 30 days of separation. These include peacemaking, peacekeeping, humanitarian, disaster relief, nation-building, and wartime deployments that fit these criteria, as well as unaccompanied tours. The measures are not perfect; the deployment counts appear to be accurate, but the months-of-deployment counts appear to have a small downward bias (see Appendix B). The measures do not include nonhostile activities of less than 30 days. Such activities involve time away from home—often for training, exercises, or routine assignment-related activities.

---

temporary relocation), and it does not identify whether the deployment involved hostile duty. The next generation of deployment data may, in effect, merge the information in the "days away" data and the PERSTEMPO data.

Chapter Four

EMPIRICAL RESULTS FROM THE REENLISTMENT MODEL

Overall, we found that nonhostile deployments increased Army, Air Force, and Marine Corps first-term reenlistment. Navy first-term reenlistment was higher for one nonhostile deployment than for none but did not rise further with more deployments. Hostile deployments had little effect on first-term reenlistment. For the most part, first-term reenlistment did not decrease with the number of hostile episodes but remained constant or slightly increased. In one case, for marines without dependents, reenlistment tended to decline as hostile deployments increased. Navy reenlistment was slightly lower for one hostile episode versus none, although it was not lower for two or more hostile episodes.

Second-term reenlistment rose with nonhostile and hostile deployments. The increase in reenlistment was greater for nonhostile deployments than it was for hostile deployments.

We also found that the effect of deployments on first-term reenlistment differed by dependency status, which mostly reflected whether a member was married or not. Members with dependents were more likely to reenlist, and their reenlistment probability rose more rapidly with nonhostile deployment. Their reenlistment was also higher for hostile deployments and showed a tendency to rise with the number of these deployments. Thus, members with dependents were more likely to reenlist at the end of the first term, and their reenlistment was higher with the greater the number of nonhostile deployments and, to a lesser extent, the greater the number of hostile deployments. These relationships help explain the similarity between the deployment and reenlistment relationship of first-term members with dependents and second-term members overall, most of whom have dependents.

Our results are conditional on the types of deployment and the deployment pays available in our study period, 1993–1999.

APPROACH

We estimated two reenlistment models, a main-effect model and a full-interaction model, by branch of service for first- and second-term reenlistment. The main-effect model contained indicator variables for one, two, or three or more nonhostile deployments and for one, two, or three or more hostile deployments. The full-interaction model created indicators for combinations of nonhostile and hostile deployment, with the omitted variable being no deployment of either type. The main-effect model fit the data better for the Army and Marine Corps, and the full-interaction model fit better for the Navy and Air Force. (Information criteria were used to judge the goodness-of-fit of the models.) The main-effect model reflects the major findings of the empirical analysis, and therefore we discuss it extensively. However, we also present results from the interaction model to show how particular combinations of deployment affect reenlistment.

We used the main-effect model to predict the effect of a 25-percent increase in deployments—all hostile. This increase is within a reasonable range for predictions because it is spread widely across members. That is, many members have no additional deployment, some have a single additional deployment, and a few have multiple additional deployments. Also, we estimated a main-effect model to determine whether the relationship between deployment and first-term reenlistment differed by dependency status.

The figures below show the predicted probability of reenlistment as a function of the number and type of deployments. The predictions were made for a member with a given set of characteristics.[1] A dif-

---

[1]These are: AFQT Category IIIA (score of 50–64), some college, electrical or mechanical equipment repairer, white male with dependents, 6.6-percent unemployment rate at prior enlistment, 4.9-percent unemployment rate at current enlistment, and FY1999.

ferent set of characteristics would change the predictions but have little effect on the shape of the relationship. Appendix C contains the sample means and standard deviations, and Appendix D contains the regression results for all models.

OVERALL RELATIONSHIP BETWEEN DEPLOYMENT AND REENLISTMENT

The predicted probabilities of reenlistment are in Figures 4.1 and 4.2 for the main-effect model and Tables 4.4 and 4.5 for the full-interaction model. The predictions are preceded by the distribution of deployment by service, term, and type of deployment in Tables 4.1 and 4.2.

Distribution of Deployment

The distribution of deployment provides some grounding for interpreting the regression results. Tables 4.1 and 4.2 show the joint distribution of hostile and nonhostile deployment for members. Many members had zero or one deployment, and relatively few had multiple deployments. Even so, we were able to estimate the effect of two or three or more deployments of either type because of our large sample.

For instance, Table 4.1 shows that 65 percent of Army first-term members had no nonhostile deployment, and 27 percent had one nonhostile deployment. The percentages for the Air Force are broadly similar to those of the Army. In comparison, 38 percent of first-term Navy members had no nonhostile deployment, and 25 percent had one nonhostile deployment. The Marine Corps percentages are similar to those of the Navy. Furthermore, the distribution of deployment for the second term (Table 4.2) was similar to that for the first term.[2]

---

[2]Because these are counts over a three-year period, the implied percentage of the force deployed in a given month is fairly small. But the dynamics of sustaining deployment can be much more demanding than a low monthly percent-deployed might suggest. Sortor and Polich (2001) find that a tempo problem can result from two sources. First, the workload caused by the combination of "war-fighting readiness, deployments, and day-to-day peacetime demands of operating a unit and installation" (p. xiii). Second, the service must cope with the dynamics of the operations, personnel

Table 4.1

Distribution of Deployment by Service, First Term (percentage)

				Hostile		
	Nonhostile	0	1	2	3+	Total
Army	0	45.73	14.74	3.40	0.64	64.52
	1	20.90	5.27	0.90	0.16	27.22
	2	5.62	1.03	0.17	0.04	6.86
	3+	1.17	0.20	0.02	0.01	1.40
	Total	73.42	21.24	4.49	0.84	100.00
Navy	0	24.18	8.64	4.99	0.67	38.49
	1	7.19	11.46	5.31	0.54	24.50
	2	6.19	9.91	4.11	0.34	20.54
	3+	7.77	6.26	2.32	0.12	16.47
	Total	45.33	36.28	16.73	1.67	100.00
Air Force	0	56.97	17.03	6.11	3.66	83.77
	1	8.96	3.01	0.95	0.37	13.29
	2	1.67	0.48	0.18	0.07	2.40
	3+	0.39	0.10	0.03	0.01	0.54
	Total	68.00	20.62	7.28	4.11	100.00
Marine Corps	0	36.88	9.03	3.91	0.56	50.39
	1	20.13	7.33	1.81	0.15	29.43
	2	12.11	2.65	0.42	0.02	15.20
	3+	4.36	0.56	0.06	0.00	4.98
	Total	73.49	19.57	6.20	0.74	100.00

SOURCE: Authors' tabulations.

management, and training systems as it seeks to "sustain the peacetime force, prepare and train for [small-scale contingency] deployments, and adhere to various peacetime operational and personnel policy constraints" (p. xiii). They conclude that the service should not focus primarily on the effect of deployment on the individual member, but "on overall force management, to evenly distribute the burden, minimize short-term readiness impacts, and ensure that longer-term skill development and war-fighting capability are sustained" (p. xiv). This recommendation is consistent with our earlier analysis (Hosek and Totten, 1998) and our current analysis.

Table 4.2

Distribution of Deployment by Service, Second Term (percentage)

			Hostile			
	Nonhostile	0	1	2	3+	Total
Army	0	45.07	13.33	3.09	0.66	62.15
	1	20.55	5.35	1.05	0.17	27.12
	2	7.41	1.40	0.22	0.03	9.06
	3+	1.35	0.28	0.04	0.00	1.67
	Total	74.38	20.36	4.40	0.86	100.00
Navy	0	50.29	9.77	2.37	0.46	62.90
	1	13.07	6.59	1.81	0.22	21.69
	2	4.44	3.79	1.09	0.10	9.42
	3+	3.04	2.25	0.67	0.05	6.00
	Total	70.84	22.40	5.94	0.83	100.00
Air Force	0	51.54	15.01	4.73	3.50	74.78
	1	12.82	4.28	1.24	0.70	19.04
	2	3.34	1.06	0.32	0.15	4.88
	3+	0.92	0.25	0.09	0.04	1.30
	Total	68.63	20.60	6.38	4.39	100.00
Marine Corps	0	38.75	5.92	1.39	0.21	46.27
	1	27.25	4.73	0.86	0.07	32.91
	2	12.69	1.93	0.12	0.00	14.75
	3+	5.34	0.58	0.14	0.00	6.07
	Total	84.04	13.17	2.51	0.28	100.00

SOURCE: Authors' tabulations.

Main-Effect Model

Figures 4.1 and 4.2 show the predicted probability of reenlistment for first- and second-term members with respect to the number and type of episodes. For the Army, Air Force, and Marine Corps, predicted first-term reenlistment increased as nonhostile episodes of deployment increased. This was consistent with the idea that members with nonhostile deployment revised their belief upward that future nonhostile deployment will be satisfying and not too frequent, and they did so with each additional nonhostile deployment.

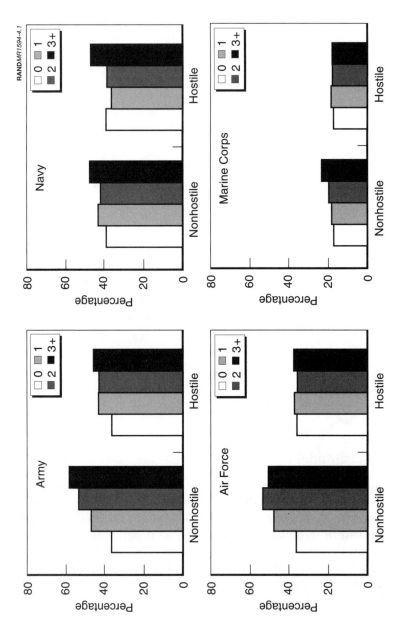

Figure 4.1—First-Term Reenlistment Probability by Number of Deployment Episodes

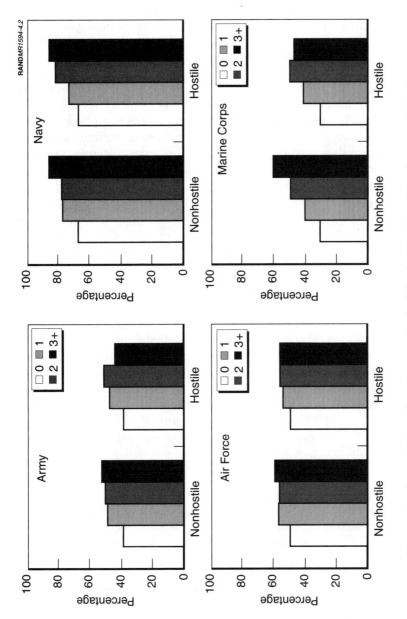

Figure 4.2—Second-Term Reenlistment Probability by Number of Deployment Episodes

Reenlistment in the Navy varied little with the number of nonhostile deployments. The type, frequency, and duration of deployment was probably more predictable in the Navy than in the other services. Many Navy deployments derive from vessels following a rotation of six months at sea and twelve months in port. The rotation was well established, so a sailor may have had little reason to revise expectations about future voyages even if deployment during the three years prior to the reenlistment decision point deviated from expectation. The results suggest that first-term sailors formed accurate expectations before their first deployment and did little subsequent updating. We show below, however, that the relationship between deployment and first-term reenlistment differed between sailors with and without dependents. Sailors with dependents had a probability of reenlistment as nonhostile deployments increased; that is, they appeared to revise their beliefs despite the predictability of Navy deployments. We think this is related, not to predictability, but to self-discovery about how much the member liked deployment.[3]

For hostile deployment, the relationship of deployment to reenlistment was largely similar across the services: Hostile deployment had little effect on reenlistment. The Army was an exception; reenlistment increased from zero to one hostile deployment and changed little thereafter. For the Navy, we found slightly lower reenlistment at one hostile deployment versus none. The findings suggest that hostile deployment, inclusive of deployment-related pay and cost, caused little net change in a member's beliefs about the satisfaction from hostile deployment. Hostile deployment may be both highly demanding and personally fulfilling. To understate, it may involve moments of extreme risk, personal loss, disease, primitive conditions, and long hours, and yet it may provide high intrinsic reward.

Second-term reenlistment (Figure 4.2) rose with nonhostile and hostile deployment up to two episodes, which encompassed most members with hostile deployment. In the Army, Marine Corps, and Air Force, there was a decrease or no increase in reenlistment with

---

[3]In terms of the functional form for utility in Chapter Two, deployment led sailors with dependents to increase values parameters a, b, c, and f through deployment, but probably not to change λ and μ.

three or more hostile deployments relative to two.[4] Members with three or more may have reached the point where hostile deployment resulted in too much time away from home, a negative impact large enough to offset the positive aspects of deployment. To state a "negative" result, we found no evidence that hostile deployment reduced reenlistment to a level below that for members who had no hostile deployment.

It is interesting to ask why there should be any effect of deployment during the second term on second-term reenlistment. Many second-term members have been promoted to the rank of a noncommissioned officer (paygrade E-5 or higher), and the satisfaction from deployment could be greater when experienced as a noncommissioned officer than as a junior enlisted member. Noncommissioned officers have leadership responsibilities and more involvement with planning and conducting missions than do junior personnel. (E-5 corresponds to a sergeant in the Army, a staff sergeant in the Air Force, a sergeant in the Marine Corps, and a petty officer second class in the Navy. The respective ranks for an E-4 are specialist, senior airman, lance corporal, and seaman.)

Also, second-term members are still learning about deployment. Even with eight or so years of service at the time of second-term reenlistment, most members have had only a few deployments. Table 4.3 shows the *unconditional* average number of deployments in the three-year period prior to reenlistment.[5] At the outset of the second term, an average member would have had roughly the average number of hostile and nonhostile deployments in the first term. Even considering hostile and nonhostile deployments together, they averaged less than one—except in the Navy, where the average was two.

---

[4]The Army coefficient for three or more hostile deployments was significantly lower than the coefficient for two hostile deployments. In the Marine Corps, these coefficients were not statistically different.

[5]The average is not conditional on the member having had some episodes.

Table 4.3

Average Number of Episodes

	First Term		Second Term	
	Hostile	Nonhostile	Hostile	Nonhostile
Army	0.33	0.45	0.42	0.50
Navy	0.76	1.25	0.50	0.61
Air Force	0.34	0.76	0.62	0.33
Marine Corps	0.50	0.20	0.32	0.82

SOURCE: Authors' tabulations.

Furthermore, second-term members are a self-selected subset of first-term members on the strength of their quality of job match with the military and preference for the military. Retention models typically assume that a member's preference, or taste, for the military is a given but unobserved factor in determining whether the member remains in service. This preference helps explain why reenlistment is higher among career members than among first-term members. But it is not obvious that a higher preference for the military leads to a positive relationship between the reenlistment probability and the *number* of deployments. If a member cannot affect deployment, there should be no relationship between preference and deployment—assuming deployment does not cause the member's preference to change. In this case, self-selection into the second term cannot explain the positive relationship between deployment and reenlistment. If the member can affect deployment, a positive relationship between deployment and reenlistment can arise if members with a stronger preference are more likely to reenlist *and* obtain more episodes. More episodes may result because the member volunteers for them or because the commanding officer selects "gung ho" members for deployment.

While that is a possibility, we return to the point that the member may still be learning about deployment. Actual deployment may shape the member's preference for the military, which can change his or her expected utility of continuing in service. If members typically find deployment to be more satisfying than expected, we will find a positive effect of deployment on reenlistment. This will be true of second-term members as well as first-term members; we expect the relationship to be stronger among second-term members because of the selectivity of first-term reenlistment. First-term members who disliked deployment presumably tend to leave the services, and second-term members who liked deployment in their first term may be deployed again in the second term and again revise their expected utility upward.

Full-Interaction Model

Tables 4.4 and 4.5 show the reenlistment probability predicted from the full-interaction model for first- and second-term reenlistment. As mentioned, the full-interaction model did not fit better than the main-effect model for the Army and Marine Corps but did for the Navy and Air Force.

For the Army first-term members, predicted reenlistment typically increased with nonhostile deployment, and it increased from zero to one hostile deployment, although the change thereafter was sporadic. Also, reenlistment decreased for three or more hostile *and* three or more nonhostile deployments, versus two hostile or two nonhostile deployments. Marine Corps first-term reenlistment tended to follow the same pattern as that of the Army.

Navy first-term reenlistment was higher for one or more nonhostile deployments compared with none, but this was true only for members who had no hostile deployments. With one or more hostile deployments, reenlistment tended to remain unchanged as nonhostile deployment increased. For members with three or more hostile deployments, reenlistment tended to decline as nonhostile deployment increased, which again was a possible sign of too much deployment. Furthermore, for one, two, or three or more nonhostile deployments, reenlistment tended to decrease as hostile deployment increased from zero to one or from one to two. The pattern for the Air Force was similar but not identical to the Navy's. Reenlistment tended to rise with nonhostile deployment and was lower for three or more hostile and three or more nonhostile deployments, compared with two hostile or two nonhostile deployments. Also, for Air Force members with one or two nonhostile deployments, reenlistment declined as hostile deployment increased from zero to one and then changed little.

Table 4.4

**Predicted First-Term Reenlistment Probability,
Full-Interaction Model**

	Nonhostile	Hostile			
		0	1	2	3+
Army	0	36.06	43.06	43.57	44.76
	1	46.84	52.57	49.57	61.20
	2	52.90	59.14	66.82	57.81
	3+	57.87	65.69	64.73	48.70
Navy	0	36.88	38.72	39.77	49.99
	1	42.88	37.60	40.28	49.14
	2	42.13	38.46	38.75	44.80
	3+	49.31	41.78	46.81	46.27
Air Force	0	35.72	37.73	36.03	37.61
	1	49.18	45.99	45.21	47.66
	2	55.31	49.28	49.78	57.53
	3+	50.45	51.70	55.03	49.31
Marine Corps	0	16.92	17.92	17.69	15.96
	1	18.02	19.04	18.44	26.12
	2	19.48	21.11	17.52	23.81
	3+	22.83	25.09	17.35	16.92

NOTE: Member has high school or some college, AFQT IIIA, electrical or mechanical equipment repairer, white, male, with no dependents, unemployment rate at prior reenlistment was 6.6 percent, current unemployment rate was 4.9 percent, and year of reenlistment decision was FY1999.

The predicted second-term Navy reenlistment probability, on a whole, rose with nonhostile and hostile deployment. Also, although reenlistment was lower among the most-deployment members versus members with two nonhostile or two hostile deployments, there was no longer a decrease in reenlistment as hostile deployment increased from zero to one or from one to two. The pattern for the Air Force was similar. In particular, among members with one, two, or three or more nonhostile deployments, there was no decrease in reenlistment as hostile deployment increased from zero to one or more deployments. Also, reenlistment was lower for the most-deployed members (three or more hostile *and* three or more nonhostile deployments). Furthermore, the patterns for the Army and Marine Corps were similar to those of the Navy and Air Force. Thus,

Table 4.5

Predicted Second-Term Reenlistment Probability, Full-Interaction Model

		Hostile			
	Nonhostile	0	1	2	3+
Army	0	38.26	48.18	51.72	47.21
	1	49.34	56.77	59.59	44.25
	2	50.32	58.23	54.75	31.60
	3+	52.53	55.15	82.55	38.26
Navy	0	66.54	75.67	86.01	90.07
	1	79.12	79.72	87.44	90.16
	2	80.72	81.29	87.12	83.60
	3+	86.51	89.04	91.7	83.27
Air Force	0	49.38	54.39	56.48	55.76
	1	57.65	59.74	63.15	67.22
	2	56.18	61.80	57.86	69.91
	3+	57.36	65.10	86.98	61.96
Marine Corps	0	29.89	39.25	58.33	45.85
	1	40.06	53.49	52.45	59.89
	2	48.65	64.76	73.70	29.89
	3+	62.96	65.53	46.04	29.89

NOTE: Member has high school or some college, AFQT IIIA, electrical or mechanical equipment repairer, white, male, with no dependents, unemployment rate at prior reenlistment was 6.6 percent, current unemployment rate was 4.9 percent, and year of reenlistment decision was FY1999.

for all services, second-term reenlistment tended to increase with nonhostile and hostile deployment, but reenlistment among the most-deployed members was lower than among members with two hostile or two nonhostile deployments.

REENLISTMENT AND DEPLOYMENT BY DEPENDENCY STATUS

We found the relationship between deployment and first-term reenlistment to differ between members with and without dependents, or put more loosely, between married and unmarried members. Compared with those without dependents, first-term members with dependents had higher reenlistment, and their reenlistment rose with nonhostile deployments and, to a lesser extent, with hostile deployments.

A possible explanation for this behavioral difference lies in the effect of deployment on the member's preference for the military. Members who discover they like deployment may also decide that the military is a preferable environment for starting and raising a family. That is, these "positive" discoveries may be correlated and affect the member's decisions to reenlist and to marry. Under this explanation, marrying is also an outcome of the learning process, and that process extends to service life overall.[6]

We considered whether the effect of deployment on reenlistment was more positive for members with dependents because they received FSA, whereas members without dependents did not. We decided FSA was likely to be a minor factor. Most deployments were less than a few months long, and FSA was $75 per month until January 1998, when it rose to $100 per month. FSA could help cover a family's deployment-related costs, but it would not appreciably change the family's standard of living.

Figure 4.3 shows predicted first-term reenlistment by dependency status; the predictions come from the main-effect model. Reenlistment was higher for members with dependents than for those without in the Navy, Air Force, and Marine Corps and about the same or perhaps slightly higher in the Army. In addition, the effect of deployment differed by dependency status (or marital status). Army reenlistment increased with nonhostile deployments, and the increase was greater for members with dependents than those without. Hostile deployments increased Army reenlistment for members with dependents. For those without dependents, reenlistment increased from zero to one hostile deployment and did not change as hostile deployments increased further. In the Navy, reenlistment for members without dependents declined slightly for zero to two nonhostile deployments. It also declined for zero to two hostile deployments but increased as deployments rose from two to three or more. Reenlistment for members with dependents increased with non-

---

[6]Future work might treat dependency status as an endogenous variable and test whether it is related to deployment.

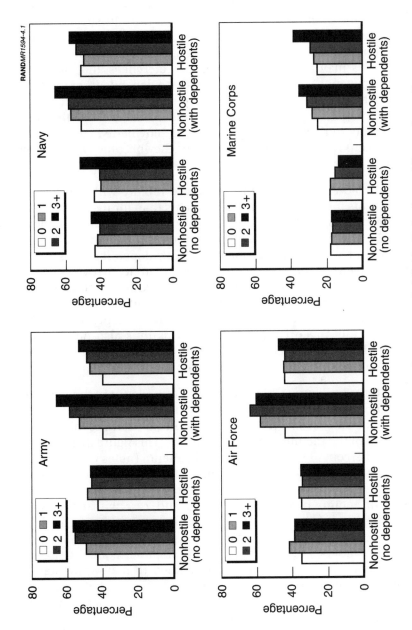

Figure 4.3—Predicted First-Term Reenlistment Probability by Episodes and Dependency Status

hostile deployments. For hostile deployment, reenlistment at first decreased and then rose. The Army and Navy results suggest that a member with dependents at the time of reenlistment had a higher expected utility of deployment than did a member without dependents. This may reflect higher revised preferences and, perhaps, higher deployment pay. Many members with dependents at the time of reenlistment might not have had dependents when deployed in the preceding three years and therefore did not receive FSA then but could expect to receive it on future long deployments. Also, sailors can expect to receive Career Sea Pay once they become eligible (see Appendix A).

In the Air Force, reenlistment rose more rapidly with nonhostile deployments for members with dependents than for members without dependents. Reenlistment did not change as hostile deployments increased for members with or without dependents, although reenlistment was higher for members with dependents (as mentioned above). In the Marine Corps, the difference between members with and without dependents is striking. Reenlistment increased with nonhostile and hostile deployment for members with dependents and decreased for members without dependents. The results for the Air Force and Marine Corps thus also point to an evolving, higher expected utility of deployment for members with dependents compared with members without dependents.

The patterns in Figure 4.3 help explain the similarity in the effect of deployment on reenlistment between first-term members with dependents and second-term members. At first-term reenlistment, about half of the members had dependents. This figure increased to about 80 percent at second-term reenlistment (Tables C.1 and C.2). The selectivity of first-term reenlistment affected the composition of second-term personnel. We found that first-term reenlistment was *higher* for members with dependents and *rose* with nonhostile deployments and, to some extent, also rose with hostile deployments. Thus, deployment was associated with a higher reenlistment rate for members with dependents. These patterns might also be present among members who soon planned to marry and start a family. As seen, the results for first-term members with dependents were largely similar to results for second-term members, with the second-term results amplifying the pattern seen for first-term members with dependents.

WHAT IF HOSTILE DEPLOYMENTS INCREASED?

We used the main-effect model to conduct a policy experiment in which deployments increased by 25 percent, and all of the new deployments involved hostile duty. The 25-percent increase is relative to a base of total deployments, so the increase is larger relative to hostile deployments. One can think of this as sustaining the level of nonhostile deployments and increasing the number of hostile deployments—e.g., peace-ops plus a new small-scale contingency.

We assumed that the hostile deployments were of the same nature as those in FY1993–FY1999 and that deployment pays and family support remained the same. We spread the additional deployments across members reenlisting in FY1999[7] via random draws from a Poisson distribution with a mean equal to 25 percent of the mean of hostile plus nonhostile deployments per member. In particular, if H was the random variable and μ was the mean number of hostile plus nonhostile deployments per member in a three-year period, then

$$\Pr(H = h) = \exp(-\lambda)\frac{\lambda^h}{h!}$$

$$E(H) = \lambda \equiv 0.25\,\mu.$$

To illustrate the values generated by this approach, suppose $\lambda = 0.25$ (and μ is assumed to equal 1). Then the probability of a member being assigned zero additional deployments is 0.7788, one additional deployment is 0.1947, two additional deployments is 0.0243, three additional deployments is 0.0020, and four additional deployments is 0.0001. More specific, Table 4.6 displays the increase in deployments. As seen, the 25-percent increase in total deployments, with all additional deployments being hostile, produced a one-third to two-thirds increase in hostile deployments, depending on the service. Within a service, the added deployments were spread randomly across members at first- and second-term reenlistment.

---

[7]The results would have been similar if we had used members reenlisting in any of our other fiscal years: 1996, 1997, or 1998.

Table 4.6

Simulated Increase in Hostile Deployments

	Initial Total Deployments	Initial Hostile Deployments	Added Hostile Deployments
Army	11,874	5,597	3,022
Navy	30,772	12,518	7,251
Air Force	14,679	11,486	3,482
Marine Corps	23,795	8,655	6,098

We found that the increase in hostile deployments had little overall effect on reenlistment for first- and second-term members (Table 4.7). In no case did the average reenlistment probability decline, and in several cases it rose slightly. This result is in keeping with the small effect of hostile deployment on reenlistment we found in the regression results. If the increase in deployments had included non-hostile deployments, the overall effect on reenlistment would have been positive, again in keeping with the regression results.

EFFECT OF OTHER EXPLANATORY VARIABLES

In our analysis, reenlistment decisions were made in the period from mid-1995 to the end of FY1999. The national economy boomed and military pay fell relative to civilian pay during this period. By the end of the 1990s, the services reported difficulty in recruiting and retention, and steps were taken to increase military pay, enlistment and reenlistment bonuses, enlistment advertising, the number of

Table 4.7

Effect on Reenlistment of Adding 25-Percent More Episodes, All Hostile

	Army	Navy	Air Force	Marine Corps
First Term				
Before	0.44	0.32	0.49	0.19
After	0.45	0.33	0.49	0.20
Second Term				
Before	0.51	0.56	0.61	0.59
After	0.53	0.58	0.61	0.61

recruiters, and the number of recruiting stations. The FY2000 National Defense Authorization Act mandated a 4.8-percent across-the-board increase in basic pay plus targeted increases that averaged out to an additional 1.4-percent increase. The Act also mandated higher-than-usual basic pay increases through FY2006.

Our data do not include enlistment or reenlistment bonus information and do not include military or civilian pay. But we used fiscal year indicators as "blunt instruments" to account for the year-to-year change in reenlistment conditions.

First-Term Reenlistment

The coefficients in the first-term main-effect model indicate that the services tended to lose high-quality members. Relative to AFQT IIIB high school graduates, the Army lost more of the highest-scoring members (AFQT I–II), kept more members with GEDs (General Equivalency Diplomas), and lost more members with some post-secondary school. The Navy lost IIIA, kept a relatively high fraction of low-scorers (AFQT IV), and kept non–high school graduates and those with GEDs. The Air Force lost AFQT I–II, AFQT IIIA, and airmen with some post-secondary education. Unlike the other services, the Marine Corps kept AFQT I–II and AFQT IIIA.

The Army and Marine Corps tended to keep women relative to men, while the Navy did not. All services had higher reenlistment rates for African Americans and Hispanics than for other (self-reported) race/ethnicity groups—primarily whites.

Members who entered when the unemployment rate was high in their state relative to other states were more likely not to reenlist, at least for the Army and Air Force. A high unemployment rate at the time of the reenlistment decision, however, made members more likely to reenlist in the Army, Air Force, and Navy (the current unemployment rate effect could not be reliably estimated for the Marine Corps). Marine reenlistment occurred on a first-come, first-served basis starting at the beginning of the fiscal year, and much of the reenlistment occurred at that time. This affected our ability to estimate the unemployment rate effect because there was little variation in the unemployment rate over the few months when much of the reenlistment occurred.

The decline in military and civilian pay in the late 1990s led us to expect that the coefficients on the fiscal year indicators would decline from one year to the next. But for the Army and Navy, the reverse was true. Most likely, these two branches managed their manpower reduction (drawdown) in the early 1990s in a way that kept first-term reenlistment rates and accessions low through FY1996, and then sought increasingly higher reenlistment rates. For the Air Force, reenlistment worsened with each passing year in the late 1990s. In managing its drawdown, the Air Force may have tried to protect all incumbent personnel and hence may have allowed first-term reenlistment to remain relatively high in FY1996. Additionally, the Air Force faced unusually strong competition from the private sector, that is, increasingly high demand for the high-aptitude, technically trained personnel the Air Force is known for. Compared with the other services, the Marine Corps' fiscal year effects were small and nearly negligible. In handling its drawdown, the Marine Corps used a "bang bang" approach and scaled down across the board in a very short period of time in the early 1990s. Thus, it was at its new steady-state personnel force structure almost immediately and, unlike the other services, did not have to cope with the ripple effects of a prolonged or shaped drawdown.

Second-Term Reenlistment

In contrast to the first-term results, second-term reenlistment rates were higher for members with higher AFQT scores and higher education. The services tended to reenlist AFQT I–II and AFQT IIIA members at a higher rate than AFQT IIIB members, and tended to shed AFQT IV members. The Navy reenlisted relatively fewer members with GEDs, and the Army, Navy, and Marine Corps kept relatively fewer non–high school graduates and relatively more members with some post-secondary education. (Air Force GED and non–high school graduate coefficients were insignificant because it had so few members with GEDs and nongraduates.)

The Army had a higher reenlistment rate for women than for men, but the Navy and Air Force had lower rates for women than for men. In every service, African Americans and Hispanics had a higher reenlistment rate than other race and ethnicity groups (again, mostly whites). In the Air Force, a higher unemployment rate at accession was associated with a lower reenlistment rate, as we expected; but in the Army and Navy, higher unemployment at accession was associated with a higher reenlistment rate. The unemployment rate at the time of reenlistment had a positive effect on reenlistment in the Air Force, also expected. But for the other services, its effect was small and insignificant; the current unemployment rate had little effect on second-term reenlistment. Finally, fiscal year effects were mostly small and insignificant. However, the Army fiscal year effect rose from FY1996 to FY1997, then declined toward the FY1996 value in FY1998–FY1999. The Marine Corps' fiscal year effects were identical in FY1996–FY1998 but lower in FY1999. In sum, there was no simple pattern to the fiscal year effects—e.g., a steady decline—and, on the whole, the fiscal year effects were small.

ADDING MONTHS OF DEPLOYMENT

The main-effect and full-interaction models used indicator variables for deployments. We realized, however, that deployments differ in length and that overall time away could affect reenlistment decisions, as the expected utility model suggests. Holding the episodes of deployment constant, lengthy deployment could cause an upward revision in the member's subjective estimate of the mean and variance of a deployment. This would affect expected utility by increasing total expected time deployed and by increasing the variance in the length of a deployment.

To allow for this, we explored models that added total months of deployment during the three-year window to our main-effect specification. In some cases, adding months had little effect on the deployment-indicator coefficients, but in other cases the coefficients changed. The intuitive explanation is both deployment indicator variables and months deployed reflect total time deployed. Nonhostile and hostile months were separately entered as a quadratic, that is, months and months squared.

Conditional on the deployment indicators, we found that reenlistment was unrelated to total nonhostile months away but was related to hostile months. We showed in Chapter Two that either a positive or negative effect of months of deployment on reenlistment was consistent with the expected utility model. We found a positive effect of months of deployment for the Army and a negative effect for the other services. Conditional on one hostile deployment, an increase from one hostile month to six hostile months changed first-term reenlistment as follows: Army, from 0.40 at one month to 0.44 at six months; Navy, from 0.39 to 0.33; Air Force, from 0.39 to 0.36; and Marine Corps, 0.19 to 0.17.[8]

This range of change in months roughly corresponds to a one-standard deviation decrease or increase from the average length of a deployment. Deployment average length and standard deviation are shown in Table 4.8. For example, the average length of a hostile deployment for first-term members in the Air Force was 3.00 months, with a standard deviation of 2.25 months.

The findings on the effect of months of deployment may be compared with tabulations from the 1999 Survey of Active Duty Personnel on the likelihood to reenlist with respect to the number of months the member was away during the year. For members who did not deploy, the likelihood to reenlist was 47 percent. This rose to 57 percent for members away less than one month, then fell gradually as follows: away one to three months, 54 percent; away four to

Table 4.8

Average Length and Standard Deviation of a Deployment

	Any Deployment		Hostile Deployment	
	Average months	Standard deviation	Average months	Standard deviation
First Term				
Army	4.6	4.1	4.6	3.1
Navy	3.8	2.6	5.5	2.3
Air Force	3.1	2.9	3.0	2.3
Marine Corps	4.5	3.1	4.7	2.9
Second Term				
Army	4.5	4.3	4.7	3.2
Navy	3.8	2.6	5.2	2.4
Air Force	3.2	3.5	2.8	2.5
Marine Corps	3.5	3.4	4.8	2.9

[8]Results are available from the authors on request.

five months, 52 percent; away five to seven months, 47 percent; and away seven to twelve months, 46 percent.[9] This is a rough comparison because the tabulations are overall, not by term or service, and do not control for member characteristics. Nevertheless, the tabulations indicate that among members with some days away during the year, the likelihood of reenlistment declines as days away increase.

In earlier work, we found a similar pattern: higher reenlistment among members with some deployment, and given some deployment, a negative effect of months deployed on reenlistment (Hosek and Totten, 1998). The results above show a negative effect of months deployed for three services, when the number of deployments is controlled. For most members, the combination of the deployments and months-of-deployment led to a higher reenlistment probability than that for members without deployment. The net positive effect on reenlistment for most members was consistent with our earlier work and with the tabulations from the 1999 survey.

CONTROLLING FOR YEARS OF SERVICE

We addressed a concern that the effect of deployment on first-term reenlistment was biased upward. The bias, if present, resulted from the likelihood that first-term members with more years of service at the reenlistment date had a stronger taste for the military and, having been in service longer, had more, and more accurately counted, deployments. Our sample population, described in Chapter Three, included members who made a reenlistment decision in FY1996–FY1999, had an initial term of 3.5 to 6.0 years, and for whom we had at least a 36-month deployment measurement window. We followed members to their final first-term decision to address the common phenomenon of extensions. Term length is chosen by the member, within the service guidelines allowed for that occupation, and therefore expresses the member's initial taste for the military. To explore the sensitivity of our models to length of initial obligation, we estimated the one-equation reenlistment model (and the two-equation model of promotion and reenlistment, discussed in the next chapter) and included a variable for length of the initial term. We

---

[9]DMDC supplied these tabulations via personal communication with the authors.

then refit these models on a smaller sample limited to members with an initial term length of 3.5 to 4.5 years.

We found that the length of the initial term was significant but had a very small effect on reenlistment. Longer initial terms were associated with higher reenlistment. Inclusion of this variable did not change the coefficients on the deployment variables. The more-selective subsample with initial terms of 3.5 to 4.5 years showed similar results, although the reduction in sample size caused some loss in statistical significance.[10]

We also reestimated the first-term reenlistment models for members with and without dependents, with the sample limited to members with initial terms of 3.5 to 4.5 years. The results were highly similar to the results discussed above.

SUMMARY

For the majority of members who had one or more nonhostile or hostile deployments in the three-year period preceding their reenlistment decision, we found that reenlistment increased as the number of nonhostile deployments increased. The exception to this pattern was the Navy, where first-term reenlistment increased from zero to one nonhostile deployment and then remained approximately constant. For hostile deployments, Army first-term reenlistment increased as hostile deployments rose from zero to one, and then stayed at about the same level. For the other services, first-term reenlistment changed little from zero to one or more hostile episodes. However, in the full-interaction model, we found that Navy and Air Force reenlistment was lower as hostile deployment increased from zero to one and one to two, for members with one or more nonhostile deployments. Among second-term members, reenlistment tended to rise with nonhostile and hostile deployments, although the increase with hostile deployments was not as rapid as with nonhostile deployments. There was little evidence that nonhostile or hostile deployment reduced first- or second-term reenlistment below the reenlistment level of members who did not deploy. However, there was evidence suggesting that the most-

---

[10]Results are available from the authors on request.

deployed members (three or more hostile deployments and three or more nonhostile deployments) had more deployment than they preferred. Their reenlistment rate was less than that of members with either two hostile or two nonhostile deployments.

In the context of the learning model and the expected utility model (Chapter Two), the results suggested that each nonhostile deployment resulted in an upward revision of expected utility. This was true for both first- and second-term members. That is, the evidence suggested that learning continued in the second term and that nonhostile deployment was a "positive" experience. Understanding precisely why this occurred is a potentially important topic for future research.

Hostile deployments seemed to bring a combination of highs and lows that resulted in little effect on reenlistment. Apart from the Army, where first-term reenlistment increased for the first hostile deployment, there appeared to be little net revision of expected utility as witnessed by the comparatively flat relationship between first-term reenlistment and hostile deployment. For second-term members, reenlistment tended to increase with hostile deployment. This suggested that among second-term members, each hostile deployment caused an upward revision of expected utility.

The second-term results revealed a more positive relationship between reenlistment and deployments for both nonhostile and hostile episodes than did the first-term results. There may be several reasons for this. Second-term members are self-selected from the first-term population; members with dependents at the end of the first term are more likely to reenlist and their reenlistment rate is higher the more deployments they had. Dependency status may be a marker for a subset of members who find military life to be satisfying in general and deployment to be satisfying in particular. Their positive reaction may be a factor in their decision to marry while serving in the military, i.e., marriage itself could be an outcome of the process of learning about their own valuation of the military. Some evidence consistent with this notion came from a comparison of the reenlistment patterns for first-term members with and without dependents. Members with dependents had reenlistment patterns similar to those of second-term members, whereas members without dependents did not. This observation is relevant because, as mentioned above, first-term members with dependents were more likely to reenlist. Equally important, their reenlistment probability was considerably higher and positively related to the number of deployments, compared with members without dependents.

In addition, second-term members typically have a higher rank than first-term members; many second-term members gain leadership responsibility as they are promoted to E-5 and become noncommissioned officers. The satisfaction from deployment may be greater as a noncommissioned officer than as an E-3 or E-4. Finally, the process of selecting members to take part in nonhostile or hostile deployments may not be completely random. To some extent, members might self-select or be selected by their commanding officer. Self-selection or commander-selection may be de facto related to the member's preference for reenlistment. If so, the relationship between reenlistment and deployment will be biased upward. If the selection process is stronger or more pervasive among second-term members than first-term members, the relationship between reenlistment and episodes will appear more positive for second-term members.

We conducted a policy experiment with the main-effect model to determine the effect of a major increase in hostile deployment on reenlistment. We predicted that a 25-percent increase in deployment, consisting entirely of hostile episodes, would have little effect on first- or second-term reenlistment. On average, reenlistment was the same or slightly higher after the increase. The experiment assumed that hostile deployments would be the same kind that occurred during our data period for counting episodes, approximately 1993–1999. Casualties and fatalities were low, and by and large the deployments were supported by the public.

Chapter Five

EMPIRICAL RESULTS FROM THE PROMOTION/ REENLISTMENT MODEL

This chapter presents selected results from the two-equation model of promotion and reenlistment with the main-effect specification. The model allows deployment to affect reenlistment directly and indirectly by affecting the expected time to E-5 that in turn affects reenlistment. The model is sequential in that time to E-5 can affect reenlistment, but reenlistment does not affect time to E-5. The model allows for error correlation between the promotion and reenlistment equations. A non-zero correlation indicates the presence of unobserved factors that affect both the time to promotion and the probability of reenlistment. Time to E-5 is measured by months in service, not months in E-4—that is, by *time in service*, not time in grade.

We found statistically significant but minor effects of deployment on the expected time to E-5. We also found a statistically significant but minor effect of expected time to E-5 on reenlistment. Therefore, the indirect effect of deployment on reenlistment via promotion was present but small. Moreover, accounting for this indirect pathway had little effect on the direct effect of deployment on reenlistment, as described in the previous chapter. As a result, the findings suggested that deployment influenced reenlistment mainly through the learning process by which the member experienced deployment and updated the expected utility of remaining in the military—in keeping with the approach presented in Chapter Two. The approach can be extended to include the probability of promotion in the expression for expected utility, but the small effects of deployment on promotion speed, and of promotion speed on reenlistment, provide little impetus for extending the model.

We also found evidence of a large, negative correlation between the promotion and reenlistment error terms. The negative correlation means that members promoted faster than expected, given their AFQT, education, occupational area, and other factors, are more likely to reenlist. The estimated value of the correlation implied a strong relationship between whether a member was promoted faster or slower than expected and the probability of reenlistment. We computed this relationship and depict it below.

We describe the services' promotion process to E-5 and then present estimates of the effect of nonhostile and hostile deployment on the expected time to E-5 promotion (measured in months). We then discuss the effect of expected time to promotion on the probability of reenlistment, and finally we discuss the promotion/reenlistment error correlation.

PROMOTION PROCESS

The following summary of the services' process for promotion to E-5 draws on Williamson (1999). Promotion depends on the accumulation of promotion points as well as the recommendation of a commanding officer or a board of selection. Every service considers a member's time in service, time in grade, physical fitness, awards and decorations, skills and knowledge, education and training, duty performance, and potential for advancement. Immediate superiors or the commanding officer assesses a member's duty performance. Importantly, the timing of promotion is related to the number of promotion points: Members who accumulate points more rapidly are promoted more rapidly.

Army

Promotion to E-5 (sergeant) is a semi-centralized process in which promotion depends on the sum of a member's administrative points and promotion selection board points. Administrative points reflect duty performance as judged by the soldier's commander, awards and decorations, military/civilian education and military training, assigned weapon qualification (expert, sharpshooter, marksman), and physical fitness scores (e.g., two-mile run, sit-ups, push-ups). The member must complete the primary leadership development course prior to promotion to E-5 but does not have to complete the course prior to being considered for promotion. The promotion selection board takes into account the soldier's personal appearance; bearing and self-confidence; oral expression and conversational skills; knowledge of basic soldiering, military programs, and world affairs; and attitude, which includes leadership, potential for advancement, and trends in performance. As of April 1994, which was close to the outset of our observations on promotion and reenlistment, a maximum of 600 administrative points and 200 board points could be awarded. Among the administrative points, the maximum number of points in each category were duty performance, 200; awards and decorations, 50; military education, 150; civilian education, 100; and military training, 100.

Navy

Navy enlisted advancement is based on Navy-wide standards and occupational standards. Specifically, promotion points depend on six factors: a standardized score on a Navy-wide advancement-in-rate examination, performance factor, time in service, time in rating (i.e., paygrade), awards, and pass-not-advanced (PNA) points. The occupational standards include personnel advancement requirements (PARS) that must be met for promotion to E-4 through E-7; PARS are numerous specific occupational skills and abilities that members must demonstrate. The Navy-wide advancement examination is given in March and September for E-4 (petty officer third class), E-5 (petty officer second class), and E-6 (petty officer first class). Candidates taking the exam in March or September are promoted in July or January, respectively, if they are selected for advancement. The number of promotions depends on the number of open positions at the higher rank. If not selected, candidates are awarded (PNA) points, and the number of PNA points depends on the average of their standardized scores over recent past exams (up to five), and on the average of their current paygrade evaluations. An average score in the upper 25 percent of scores receives 1.5 PNA points, as does an average performance mark in the upper 25 percent. Being in the next 25 percent merits 1.0 PNA point, and being in the next 25 percent merits 0.5 PNA point.

Air Force

Promotion to E-5 (staff sergeant) in the Air Force is based on a centralized system that takes into account time in service, time in grade, skill level, promotion points, and the recommendation of the member's commanding officer. Air Force specialties typically have five skill levels: 1 (helper), 3 (apprentice), 5 (journeyman), 7 (craftsman), and 9 (superintendent). In moving from one skill level to the next, the airman must satisfy requirements for career knowledge, job proficiency, and job experience. On-the-job training programs satisfy the requirements for career knowledge and job proficiency, and satisfactory job performance over a minimum specified time period satisfies the job experience requirement. Most promotions to E-5 through E-7 occur under the weighted airman promotion system (WAPS), and others occur under stripes for exceptional performance (STEP). The WAPS score depends on a weighted sum of six factors. The factors and their relative weights are: specialty knowledge test (SKT) score, 0.22; promotion fitness examination (PFE), 0.22; time in service, 0.09; time in grade, 0.13; decorations, 0.05; and performance reports, 0.29. The SKT and PFE are multiple-choice tests that measure career field knowledge and knowledge of military subjects and management practices, respectively. The performance evaluation report addresses conduct, performance, knowledge of duties, communications skills, supervisory and leadership abilities, and compliance with standards and training requirements. There are at least two evaluators who are typically the airman's immediate superiors. The commander reviews all performance reports and makes a recommendation regarding promotion. The review includes all reports, up to ten, within the past five years to compute the performance report score. Reports are weighted so that more-recent reports receive more weight.

Under the STEP program, an airman may be promoted at the discretion of commanders of major commands, field operating agencies, and senior officers of organizations with large enlisted populations. However, only a limited number of STEP promotions may be made. Also, an airman must have at least three years in service and complete the Airman Leadership School for promotion to E-5.

Promotion to E-5 has historically taken longer in the Air Force than in the other services. Among members who reached E-5 and were in service at a given point in time, airmen typically took two years longer to reach E-5 than did members of the other services.

Marine Corps

Promotions to E-5 (sergeant) are based on time in service, time in grade, composite score (CS), and the recommendation of a selection board. The composite score is a computation based on rifle marksmanship, physical fitness, average duty proficiency, average conduct, and bonus points awarded for being a drill instructor, recruiter, or Marine Security Guard; for self-education since last promotion; or for participation in the command recruiting program for referrals of new recruits. The commander determines the marine's average duty proficiency through observation, interview, and proficiency marks in the lower grades. Selection boards meet annually to consider each marine's fitness for promotion. The boards consider achievement, leadership, types and levels of experience, professional and technical knowledge, growth potential, motivation, general military proficiency, personal appearance, special qualifications (such as language skills), physical condition, moral character, and maturity. Marines selected for promotion are promoted throughout the year as openings occur at the higher grade by primary occupational specialty. Among selected marines, promotion depends on the CS, which is computed quarterly.

Table 5.1

Time in Service and Time in Grade Requirements for E-5

	Army	Navy	Air Force	Marine Corps
Time in service (TIS)	3 years	3 years	3 years	2 years
TIS waiverable[a]	18 months	n/a	n/a	18 months
Time in grade (TIG) E-4 (months)	8 months	12 months	6 months	12 months
TIG waiverable	4 months	n/a	n/a	n/a

[a]For the Marine Corps, 18 months is the minimum time in service for a "merit promotion" to E-5.

Finally, to be specific about the time in service and time in grade requirements for E-5, we again drew upon Williamson (1999) to prepare Table 5.1.

EFFECT OF DEPLOYMENT ON EXPECTED TIME TO E-5

The deployment variables in the time–to–E-5 regressions for first- and second-term reenlistment (see Tables D.7 and D.8, respectively) provide estimates of the increase or decrease in months to promotion.[1] These coefficients are from a promotion regression that controls for AFQT category, education level, speed to E-4 (by quartile, e.g., upper one-fourth), occupational area, fiscal year, and calendar quarter of entry into service. The calendar quarter of entry controls for the unevenness of accessions during the year. In quarters where accessions are high, the number of members later competing for a promotion will be high, which we hypothesize could lengthen a member's expected time to promotion.

The deployment coefficients from Table D.7 are plotted in Figure 5.1. As seen, nonhostile episodes reduced the expected time to promotion by two to six months in the Army as deployment increased from zero to three or more episodes. In the Navy and Air Force, nonhostile deployment reduced expected time to promotion by two to three months, compared with having no nonhostile deployment. However, the reduction in time to promotion did not significantly change with the number of episodes. For the Marine Corps, the reduction was present but small: less than a month for marines with one or two nonhostile deployments. With respect to hostile deployment, the effects on time to promotion are also small. In the Army, one hostile deployment barely changed the expected time to promotion, while two hostile deployments lengthened it by less than a month, and three or more lengthened it by about two months. All the effects in the Navy were small: plus or minus less than one month. In the

---

[1]In the first-term model, time to E-5 was treated as a censored variable if the member did not reenlist or had not reached E-5 before the end of the observation period. Otherwise, the time to E-5 was observed prior to reenlistment or, more often, in the second term after reenlistment. In the second-term model, time to E-5 was observed for most members but was censored if the member had not reached E-5 before the end of the observation period.

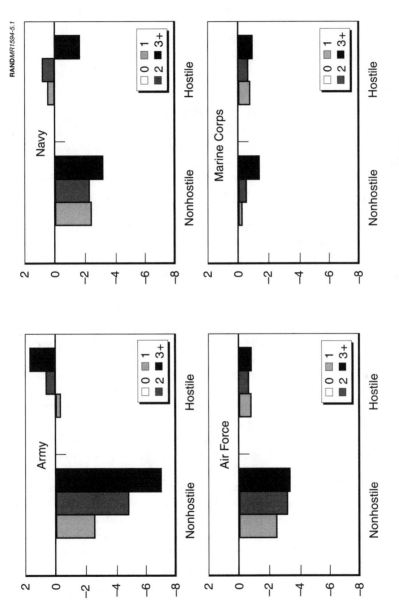

Figure 5.1—Predicted Change in Months to E-5 Promotion by Number of Deployments

Air Force and Marine Corps, the effects were uniformly negative—hostile episodes reduced time to E-5—but less than a month. Because many members in the Army, Navy, and Marine Corps do not reach E-5 until the fifth or sixth year of service, a reduction of one or two months must be considered small. This observation applies more strongly to the Air Force, where E-5 is reached in the seventh or eighth year of service.

The estimates from Table D.8 generally tell the same story, namely, that nonhostile deployment reduced expected time to E-5 but the effects were small, usually less than a month or two. Hostile episodes also had small effects, around one month but sometimes larger, and they increased time to E-5 in the Army and Air Force but reduced it in the Navy and Marine Corps. Thus, whether we examined the deployment effects on time to E-5 promotion from Tables D.7 or D.8, we found that nonhostile episodes of deployment reduced expected time to E-5, but the effect was small and probably of little policy significance. Hostile episodes tended to have even smaller effects, and although the effects were sometimes positive and sometimes negative, the small size suggests that they also were of little consequence.

EFFECT OF EXPECTED TIME TO E-5 ON REENLISTMENT

Table 5.2 presents estimates of the effect of expected time to E-5 on the first- and second-term probability of reenlistment, based on Tables D.7 and D.8. The reenlistment regressions contained the explanatory variables present in the one-equation model of reenlistment, plus a variable for the member's expected time to E-5 based on the promotion equation. The other variables controlled for the member's deployment, AFQT category, education level, occupational area, race/ethnicity, gender, dependency status, unemployment rate, and fiscal year. Thus, the estimated effect of expected time to E-5 on the probability of reenlistment indicated whether, say, a longer expected time to promotion made the member less likely to reenlist, with other factors constant. This was indicated by a negative coefficient.

The coefficients in Table 5.2 did not reveal any strong pattern of expected time to E-5 affecting the probability of first- or second-term

Table 5.2

Effect of Expected Time to E-5 Promotion on Reenlistment

	Army	Navy	Air Force	Marine Corps
First Term				
Coefficient	0.0091	−0.5374	0.1153	−0.0328
Standard error	(0.0012)	(0.0802)	(0.0265)	(0.0007)
Second Term				
Coefficient	−0.0116	−0.0380	−0.0062	0.0185
Standard error	(0.0040)	(0.0111)	(0.0036)	(0.0053)

NOTE: All coefficients are statistically significant at 0.01 except the second-term Air Force coefficient, which is significant at 0.10. Standard errors are in parentheses.

enlistment. Five of the eight coefficients were negative, as expected, but three were positive. The first-term Army and Air Force results may be compared with Buddin et al. (1992, pp. 31, 55), who found that longer expected time to E-5 promotion had a negative effect on first-term reenlistment for Army and Air Force members in the mid-1980s. In contrast, we found positive effects in these cases.

Although all the coefficients in Table 5.2 were statistically significant, many of the coefficients were small in absolute size. This implied that, given the small effect of deployment on expected time to E-5, the effect of deployment on reenlistment via promotion was small and of little policy significance. The Army first-term coefficient, 0.0091, implied that a two-month reduction in expected time to E-5 reduced the probability of reenlistment by about −0.006. Only the first-term Navy and Air Force coefficients were "large." The Navy coefficient, −0.5374, was the largest compared with the other coefficients, but time units for the Navy were six months long. (Navy promotions occur every six months in July and January.) We divided the coefficient by six to put it on a monthly basis, which yielded an estimate of −0.09. Referring back to Figure 1.1, the Navy first-term reenlistment probability was in the neighborhood of 0.30 to 0.35, so a one-month decrease in expected time to E-5 increased the probability by about 0.033, a 10-percent increase.[2] For the Air Force, a longer

---

[2]In the probit model $\partial P / \partial x_i = \phi(x'\beta)\beta_i$. At an initial value of P equal to 0.35 and β_i equal to −0.09, $\partial P / \partial x_i$ equals 0.033.

expected time to E-5 promotion increased the first-term reenlistment probability; the coefficient was 0.1153. Given a first-term reenlistment probability of about 0.50, a one-month increase in expected time to promotion increased probability by 0.046, a 9-percent increase.

ERROR CORRELATION

We found the error correlation between promotion and reenlistment to be negative. This indicated the presence of unobserved factors that reduced time to E-5 promotion and increased the probability of reenlistment. We could not identify the factors, but we believe they reflect ability, taste for the military, and effort. Taken singly, it is not clear any of these factors would induce a correlation between promotion and reenlistment. High-ability members are more likely to be promoted fast, even if their effort is average.[3] But ability itself may have little bearing on a member's willingness to reenlist. High-taste members are more likely to reenlist, but taste itself may have little effect on a member's performance, fitness, awards, education and training, and, hence, on promotion speed. Effort level will presumably depend on the perceived reward, which may depend on whether effort can bring better assignments and faster promotion. We speculate that effort and ability interact; high ability should reduce the effort required to complete a task and facilitate the development of abstract skills that are valued in promotion such as leadership, resource allocation, and decisionmaking under uncertainty (e.g., in a wartime environment). Effort and taste may interact. Greater taste for the military implies a higher personal value on staying and, thus, higher reward from effort. So high-taste members may exert more effort, which should reduce time to E-5, and are also more likely to reenlist. Ability complements the interaction between taste and effort; high ability reduces the effort required per task and increases the potential range of attainment.

---

[3]Recall that the promotion regression controls for AFQT and speed to previous promotion, E-4. So unobserved ability captures some additional aspect of ability. Furthermore, because of the possibility that time to E-4 might be correlated with unobserved ability, we estimated models that excluded the time–to–E-4 variables. However, this produced little change in the coefficient and correlation estimates, indicating that our results were not sensitive to the inclusion of time to E-4.

However, ability can also be expected to support better job prospects outside the military. Therefore, although ability can assist high-taste members who are willing to make the effort required to perform well in the military, ability alone is unlikely to be the source of the negative error correlation.

Table 5.3 shows the estimated error correlation between time to E-5 promotion and first- and second-term reenlistment.[4]

The first-term correlation for the Army, Navy, and Marine Corps was around –0.30, but the Air Force's was near zero at –0.06. The second-term estimates were just under –0.5 for the Army, Navy, and Air Force and about –0.2 for the Marine Corps. Although the second-term estimates were larger in absolute value for three of the services, this probably resulted from the second-term population being a selected subset of the first-term population. Also, the Air Force second-term estimate was about the same as that of the Army and Navy, suggest-

Table 5.3

Error Correlation Between Time to E-5 Promotion and Reenlistment

	Army	Navy	Air Force	Marine Corps
First Term				
Coefficient	–0.3460	–0.3234	–0.0661	–0.2894
Standard error	(0.0072)	(0.0084)	(0.0146)	(0.0063)
Second Term				
Coefficient	–0.4921	–0.4366	–0.4810	–0.2214
Standard error	(0.0070)	(0.0083)	(0.0049)	(0.0176)

NOTE: Each correlation is significant at 0.01.

---

[4]We applied the same two-equation promotion/reenlistment model to second-term reenlistment as we did to first-term reenlistment. Because the second-term population is a self-selected subset of the first-term population, this selectivity can be expected to affect the estimate of the correlation. That is, the error correlation in the second-term model is conditional on first-term reenlistment. Future work should consider a three-equation (or alternative) model that treats time to E-5, first-term reenlistment, and second-term reenlistment in a unified way.

ing a similar underlying selection process, even though the Air Force first-term correlation was small.[5]

A correlation of –0.3 implies a strong relationship between the time to E-5 and the probability of reenlistment after controlling for the observed explanatory variables. We computed the probability of reenlistment as a function of time to E-5, given an error correlation of –0.3, and show the relationship in Figure 5.2.[6]

The figure plots the probability of reenlistment conditional on the extent to which time to E-5 is faster or slower than expected, given the member's explanatory variables. The latter, on the x-axis, is measured in units of the standard deviation of time to promotion. If the member's time to E-5 equals the expected time to E-5, given the

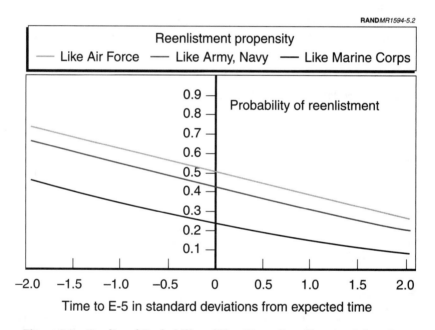

Figure 5.2—Predicted Probability of First-Term Reenlistment When E-5 Promotion Is Slower or Faster Than Expected (error correlation –0.3)

---

[5]Buddin et al. (1992, pp. 31, 55) found an error correlation of –0.09 for the Army and –0.29 for the Air Force in data from 1983–1989.

[6]The computation is available from the authors on request.

member's AFQT, education level, and so forth, then the member's value on the x-axis is zero. If time to E-5 is one standard deviation longer to E-5 than expected, the value on the x-axis is one. The three curves in the figure reflect different propensities to reenlist. The upper line depicts a propensity to reenlist like that of airmen, the middle line like that of soldiers and sailors, and the lower line like that of marines. We can think of the x-axis as describing the member's private knowledge about his anticipated time of promotion relative to that of observationally equivalent peers (having the same AFQT, education, occupation, etc.). We add this point because the probability of reenlistment can depend on the member's anticipated time to promotion. Although promotion has not yet occurred, the member may have a clear sense of being ahead of, or behind, the pack.

As seen, a member with a reenlistment probability of 0.5 when time to E-5 is at par (zero on the x-axis) will have a reenlistment probability above 0.6 if time to E-5 is one standard deviation faster than expected. The reenlistment probability will be below 0.4 if time to E-5 is one standard deviation slower than expected. The comparisons for the other curves are similar. To a first approximation, on any of the curves, a one-standard deviation increase or decrease in time to E-5 reduces or increases the probability of reenlistment by 0.10. These are significant changes.

Tables D.7 and D.8 indicate that the standard deviation of the error of time to E-5 is about 18 months for the Army, 19 months for the Navy, 15 months for the Air Force, and 8 months for the Marine Corps. Given a member's explanatory variables and the assumption of our model that the error terms are normally distribution, we expect about 19 percent of members to have a time to E-5 promotion between zero and one-half standard deviation faster than expected. About 15 percent have a promotion between one-half and one standard deviation faster than expected, and about 16 percent have a promotion more than one standard deviation faster than expected. From Figure 5.2, we judge that the 15 percent between one-half and one standard deviation faster have a probability of reenlistment of 0.05 to 0.10 higher than someone promoted at par. The 16 percent with even faster promotions have a probability of reenlistment at more than 0.10 higher. Given that the same sort of comparisons apply to promotions that are slower than par, it is clear that the extent to which (anticipated) time to E-5 promotion is faster or slower than expected powerfully differentiates those who will reenlist from those who will not.

EFFECT OF OTHER VARIABLES ON PROMOTION

We found that higher AFQT and higher education reduced the time to E-5 promotion, as expected. Also, a shorter time to E-4 was associated with a shorter time to E-5 in the Army, Navy, and Marine Corps. For example, in the Army reaching E-4 in the fastest quartile was associated with reaching E-5 14 months sooner than in the slowest quartile. Similarly, reaching E-4 in the second- and third-fastest quartiles was associated with reaching E-5 8.6 and 5.6 months sooner, respectively.[7] In the Marine Corps, marines in the fastest, second-fastest, and third-fastest quartiles to E-4 could expect promotion 21, 15, and 9 months sooner to E-5 than marines in the slowest quartile. For the Navy, we found that sailors whose time to E-4 was faster than the median time could expect to be about two months faster to E-5 than those slower to the median time. Thus, in the Army and Marine Corps, and to a lesser extent in the Navy, a fast time to E-4 was associated with a fast time to E-5. In other words, the gain from reaching E-4 sooner was at least partially conserved in that E-5 was also reached sooner.

Whereas the difference in months to E-5 between time–to–E-4 quartiles was often more than several months in the Army and Marine Corps, the difference in the Air Force was much smaller (one to four months). In addition, the Air Force had an anomalous result: compared with airmen in the slowest quartile of time to E-4, airmen in any faster quartile had a slightly *longer* time to E-5 promotion. We do not know why. We constructed the time–to–E-4 quartiles from a longitudinal database of *all* enlisted members, tracking them *by cohort* from the time of accession (entry into service) to the time of promotion to E-4. We limited our tabulation of time to E-4 quartiles

---

[7]These Army estimates are from the time to E-5/first-term reenlistment model. The estimates from the time to E-5/second-term reenlistment model are somewhat different. The coefficients for the top, second, and third quartile of time to E-4 indicate promotion times 11.0 months, 4.5 months, and 1.3 months shorter than for the fourth (slowest) quartile to E-4, respectively. Still, the basic story is the same. This point holds for the other services as well.

to members who stayed in service long enough to reach E-4, that is, members for whom time to E-4 was realized. This was done by narrowly defined (three-digit) occupational specialty. Therefore, the Air Force result does not reflect differences in speed of promotion across occupations, as might have been the case if we had pooled data across specialties when computing time–to–E-4 quartiles. Instead, we speculate that airmen who were slow to E-4 but strove to improve and stayed in the Air Force were able to obtain large improvements in their performance relative to their peers; this led to a somewhat faster time to E-5 than their peers. Another possibility is that airmen who were fast to E-4 were somewhat slow to E-5 because they had to be in service long enough to satisfy the time-in-service requirement. However, this seems unlikely because the TIS requirement is only three years (see Table 5.1).

The range of time to E-5 across broad occupational areas was about six months in the Army and Navy, three months in the Air Force, and two months in the Marine Corps (see the occupational area coefficients in Table D.7). A two- to three-month range is small relative to the five or more years needed to reach E-5.

In most cases, the calendar quarter of accession made little difference in time to E-5. The indicator variables for the second, third, and fourth quarter were usually statistically significant for the Army and Air Force but not for the Navy and Marine Corps. But, the coefficients were nearly always small—for example, less than one month. The fiscal year effects were also minor.

SUMMARY

The analysis of promotion and reenlistment revealed a statistically significant but small negative effect of nonhostile episodes on the time to E-5 promotion. For members with one nonhostile deployment, for example, E-5 promotion occurred a month or two sooner than for members with no nonhostile deployment. For members who had two or more nonhostile deployments, promotion was a bit faster, especially in the Army. The effect of hostile deployment on time to E-5 promotion was smaller than for nonhostile deployment. Unlike nonhostile deployment, which generally shortened the time to E-5, hostile deployment sometimes shortened the time and sometimes lengthened it. Regardless, the effect on time to E-5 was typically less than one month and therefore of little practical significance.

We also found that the expected time to E-5 promotion in most cases had a small effect on the probability of first- or second-term reenlistment. As a result, the small change in expected time to E-5 resulting from nonhostile or hostile episodes had a small, perhaps negligible, effect on reenlistment. The empirical evidence pointed to the conclusion that deployments had little effect on reenlistment via their effect on the time to E-5 promotion. Furthermore, allowing for this effect did not dislodge the finding in the previous chapter that deployment had a direct effect on first- and second-term reenlistment. The direct-effect estimates in the promotion/reenlistment model were similar to the direct-effect estimates in the one-equation reenlistment model.

Our findings on the error correlation between promotion and reenlistment reflect the presence of unobserved factors that acted to reduce time to E-5 promotion and increase reenlistment. These factors involve an interaction of a member's *taste* for the military, *effort* to perform, and *ability*, which can reduce the effort needed to accomplish tasks and acquire the skills and knowledge needed for career advancement. Controlling for such observed characteristics as AFQT category, education, speed to E-4, and occupational area, we found that a member who is one standard deviation faster (slower) to E-5 has a first-term reenlistment probability 0.10 higher (lower) than a member whose promotion occurs no sooner or later than expected. The unobserved factors therefore had a large influence on who continued in service beyond the first term.

Although taste, effort, and ability are difficult to observe and measure, the promotion system can give a net indication of their effect. After taking account of members' observed characteristics, a commanding officer should expect that members accumulating promotion points more rapidly are the ones more likely to be promoted sooner *and to reenlist*. That is, promotion point accumulation may be thought of as a signal of the net effect a member's taste, effort, and ability.

Chapter Six

CLOSING THOUGHTS

REFLECTIONS ON THE FINDINGS

Our analysis was motivated by concern that today's heightened pace of peacetime deployments placed an unusually heavy burden on military personnel, one large enough to reduce reenlistment. However, the results of our empirical analysis provided little support for this view. To conduct our analysis, we focused on active-duty enlisted members and counted a member's nonhostile and hostile episodes of deployment over a three-year period ending three months prior to the date when the member made a decision to reenlist or to leave military service. The members in this count had initial terms of service of three and a half years or more. For first-term members, we found that reenlistment rose with the number of nonhostile deployments and typically was little affected by the number of hostile deployments. For second-term members, we found that reenlistment rose with nonhostile and hostile deployments. The rise was more rapid for nonhostile episodes than for hostile episodes. Rather than decreasing reenlistment, deployment generally served to increase it or leave it unchanged.

Our analysis was also motivated by the question of why past deployment might affect a member's reenlistment decision. In what way did the past shape current decisionmaking? We explored two hypotheses: the learning hypothesis and the promotion hypothesis. The learning hypothesis assumes that a member learns about the satisfaction (or dissatisfaction) of deployment through actual deployment. Although a member enters service with expectations about whether deployment will be satisfying, these are naive expectations. There are few, if any, civilian-life counterparts to military deployment. We presented a model of Bayesian updating as a mechanism of learning about deployment. We also described how a deployment can alter a member's expected utility of continuing in the military, where expected utility depends on the member's possible changing preferences for deployment and on deployment pays and costs. If deployment leads to an increased value of expected future utility, the member is more likely to reenlist.[1]

The promotion hypothesis assumes that past deployment can affect reenlistment by changing the time to promotion. Faster promotion means higher pay and a more rapid career advancement, and, hence, higher expected utility. We focused on promotion to the first non-commissioned officer rank, paygrade E-5, which some members reach in their first term, but most reach in their second term. We assumed that the promotion system was stable and that members understood it well, so a member could gauge how fast he or she would be promoted.

Our findings were consistent with the learning hypothesis and the promotion hypothesis. However, the promotion effects were small and of little practical significance. Thus, the promotion hypothesis did not appear to be a major explanation of why past deployment affects reenlistment decision. The learning hypothesis permits past deployment to have a negative, positive, or zero effect on reenlistment; it is a means of incorporating experience into decisionmaking. Our finding that reenlistment rose with the number of nonhostile deployments is consistent with the notion that each nonhostile episode was a positive experience that induced an upward revision in the expected utility of remaining in the military. The finding among first-term members that reenlistment was largely unaffected by hostile deployment is consistent with the view that such episodes

---

[1]Members may have any variety of utility functions. For example, a member may enter the military on a "vision quest" seeking to test his or her mettle in a hostile deployment, or he or she may want to make some positive if finite patriotic contribution and then leave. Wardynski (2000, p. 141) raised these possibilities in his discussion of how deployment might affect reenlistment.

involve more-extreme risks, hardships, and rewards that lead to little net change in expected utility.[2,3]

The learning model allows preferences for deployment to differ across members. As members learn about the utility they derive from the military and from deployment, they may make significant decisions in their life. We found that members who were married (i.e., had dependents) by the time of the reenlistment decision were more likely to reenlist and had a larger, positive effect of deployment on reenlistment than did members who were not married. This was true at both first- and second-term reenlistment. It did not mean that deployment "caused" marriage, but rather that the type of member who derived satisfaction from the military and from deployment was also the type more likely to marry in service. In other words, dependency status revealed type: The type of member to marry also tended to like the military, deployment, and would likely reenlist. Some members of this type were not married at the end of the first term, and therefore their type had not yet been revealed. These members were presumably likely to marry in the second term; in fact, many members (about three-fourths) were married by the end of the second term. If this type was more likely to reenlist, it is not surprising to find a strong similarity between the effect of deployment on reenlistment for first-term members with dependents and on second-term reenlistment in general.

Finally, we found a large negative error correlation between promotion and reenlistment. The unobserved factors implied by this correlation strongly influence the probability of reenlistment. We estimated that being one standard deviation faster or slower than expected to E-5 promotion led to an increase or decrease in the reenlistment probability of plus or minus 0.10. The unobserved factors may represent the interplay of taste for the military, effort, and

---

[2]As mentioned earlier, our findings reflect the effect of the deployments per se as well as deployment pay and costs. In particular, the findings are conditional on deployment pay as it existed in our study period. (It is much the same today.)

[3]The findings do not seem consistent with a vision-quest hypothesis because it suggests that a member who experienced hostile deployments would be less likely to reenlist. The findings also do not seem consistent with the onetime patriotic-contribution hypothesis, because members with more deployments were usually more likely, not less likely, to reenlist.

ability. Members with a high taste for the military may exert more effort to gain promotion, and high ability enables higher performance for a given amount of effort. By looking at a member's rate of accumulation of promotion points relative to that of his or her peers, after controlling for observed characteristics, a service can identify the members likely to reach E-5 faster and those more likely to reenlist.

DIRECTIONS FOR FUTURE RESEARCH

We found that nonhostile deployments had a positive effect on reenlistment. These deployments consist of absences of 30 days or more for such purposes as humanitarian aid, disaster relief, nation-building, lengthy exercises or training events, and unaccompanied tours. But apart from this simple listing, we do not know why these deployments were more satisfying than members expected, that is, why they apparently led to an upward revision of the expected utility of continuing in the military. What were the member's initial expectations, how were they formed, and what aspects of nonhostile deployment led to an upward revision? Why did the effect of deployment differ between members with dependents and those without? To what extent were deployments not exogenous to the member but determined by self-selection or commander selection, and did that interact with dependency status?

Similarly, we found that hostile deployments, such as peacemaking and peacekeeping operations, had little effect on reenlistment, but we do not know what elements of these experiences were typically positive or negative or what, if anything, might be done to improve the satisfaction from these experiences. The data did not contain information about the purpose, location, conditions, risks, challenges, rewards, and costs of the deployment, as seen from the member's perspective. Furthermore, we have little idea of how deployment, whether hostile or nonhostile, affected friends and family—particularly the spouse of a deployed member. Although there is some information on this, we do not know how family and friends mediate the member's response to deployment. For instance, does lengthy deployment result in greater financial stress and indebtedness for the young military family?[4]

Our deployment database did not contain information on short (less than 30 days) nonhostile deployments. The hostile deployment indicator denoted any hostile deployment in a month, but it did not specify the length or number of hostile deployments in the month. The count of months of deployment could be made more accurate by using data on the amount of deployment pay received, not just whether it was received. We think that "merging" the PERSTEMPO data and new "days away" data could improve the scope and accuracy of deployment data; each data set has something to contribute. Also, adding information about the geographic origin and destination of deployment would enable analysts to test whether deployments from certain areas were adverse.[5] Likewise, it would be useful to identify the type of deployment. A starting point for the typology of deployment would be: peacemaking, peacekeeping, humanitarian assistance, disaster relief, nation-building, border patrol, major exercise, education or training, unaccompanied tour of duty, or other. It would also be valuable to have a name or identifier for the specific operation, if applicable, and a related database that described the operation in some detail, including quality-of-life aspects.[6]

Finally, we suggest broadening the analysis of deployment to include first-term attrition. Studies of the effect of deployment on reenlistment, including this one, focus on members at the time of reenlist-

---

[4]Tiemeyer, Wardynski, and Buddin (1999, p. 15). Data from a 1997 RAND survey of enlisted career intentions found overall that members who had recently been deployed did *not* have a greater incidence of financial difficulties than their peers who had not been deployed. But this study recommended further analysis to see if deployment-related financial difficulties were present in particular groups, e.g., junior enlisted members with wives and children.

[5]In recent unpublished work, Wardynski reported a lower reenlistment among Army members deployed from Asia, compared with members who did not deploy. He also found a higher reenlistment if members were deployed from Europe or the United States, provided the deployment was not too long. His research focused specifically on the effect of hostile deployment on the first-term reenlistment of single Army members. (Personal communication with the authors.)

[6]According to a General Accounting Office (GAO) report, the Army has spent over $2 billion to "build camps and implement services" in the Balkans since December 1995. The GAO found that "most soldiers were satisfied with the living conditions and recreational facilities" (GAO, 2000; quotes from report abstract).

ment, but approximately 30 percent of new recruits do not complete their first term of service. It remains to be seen whether deployment is a factor in their departure, and whether formally controlling for attrition affects the estimated effect of deployment on first-term reenlistment. A deployment analysis that follows a member from entry through the first term and possibly beyond requires longitudinal data as well as longitudinal theoretical and empirical models of retention.

DEPLOYMENT-RELATED PAY

Pays include Basic Allowance for Subsistence (BAS), Family Separation Allowance (FSA), Hostile Fire/Imminent Danger Pay (abbreviated here as HFP), awards for extending an overseas tour, an exclusion from the withholding of federal and state income tax for duty in combat zones, Career Sea Pay and Career Sea Pay Premium, and Hardship Duty Pay.[1] Most personnel who go on long or hostile duty are eligible for at least one of these pays. Our discussion concentrates on deployment-related pays as they existed during our study window, which covers deployments from 1993 through 1999.[2]

We first describe the pays and conclude with a table summarizing pays a member might receive when deployed. The purpose of this discussion is to highlight the existence and amounts of these pays, which in general help to compensate for the separation, poor conditions, danger, and arduous duty that may come with deployment. The pays probably play an important role in compensating for adverse aspects of deployment. However, because there was little change in the amounts or eligibility conditions for these pays during our study period, we cannot empirically identify the effects of these pays on a member's decision to reenlist.

---

[1]The source for the material in this appendix is: Under Secretary of Defense (Comptroller), *Military Pay Policy and Procedures: Active Duty and Reserve Pay*, Volume 7A, updated June 5, 2001. It may be accessed online at www.dtic.mil/comptroller/fmr/07a.

[2]A recent addition to the deployment-related pays discussed here is the "deployment per diem," which would pay $100 per day to members away from home more than 400 days in a two-year period.

BASIC ALLOWANCE FOR SUBSISTENCE

The Gulf War prompted two major provisional changes in eligibility for BAS.[3] Subsequent legislation made these changes permanent as of January 1, 1998. First, enlisted members being "subsisted in kind" became entitled to receive a partial BAS, except during basic training. (BAS is payable on a daily basis to enlisted personnel.) This increased the number of personnel receiving BAS, although the amount of BAS was small. Second, enlisted members temporarily assigned to duty away from their permanent duty station become entitled to BAS at a rate not less than that at their permanent duty station.

A member deployed for temporary duty receives a per diem that is intended to cover food, lodging, and incidentals. If the deployed member receives food and lodging in kind, the per diem allocations for food and lodging are automatically subtracted from the per diem, leaving a small amount for incidentals ($3.50 per day). Before the Gulf War, a member receiving full BAS would lose that amount when on temporary duty, assuming he or she received government-provided meals on that duty. The changes brought by the Gulf War allowed the member to keep full BAS; the cost of food and lodging was debited from the member's per diem. The underlying principle now at play is that the member, when deployed on temporary duty, continues to receive no less BAS than when he or she is not deployed.

Officers already had been entitled to BAS at all times on a monthly basis. In addition, commanders often granted permission to enlisted personnel to "mess separately," depending on such factors as the location of a member's residence, specialized duties, working hours, dining hall capacity, or distance to the mess hall. As a result, many enlisted personnel with dependents who lived off base could receive Separate Rations (SEPRATS), that is, BAS to compensate for messing separately. There were no changes to officers' entitlement to BAS or in granting SEPRATS to enlisted members.

As of January 1, 2001, enlisted members receive $0.86 per day for partial BAS, which is the equivalent of $25.80 for a 30-day month.

------

[3]We are grateful to CMDR Kevin Harkins, OSD(P&R), for conferring with us on the interpretation of the BAS provisions.

But as of January 1, 2002, enlisted members on partial BAS will receive full BAS when deployed. Enlisted members on SEPRATS (full BAS) receive $7.66 per day, the equivalent of $229.80 for a 30-day month. Officer BAS is $160.42 per month. The meal collection rates for members receiving full BAS are $6.60 per day for discounted meals (or $198 for a 30-day month) and $8.00 per day for meals that are not discounted (or $240 for a 30-day month). The discount rate applies to sea duty or temporary afloat assignment as well as to field duty or temporary field assignment. Again, meal costs for personnel on temporary duty are covered by the per diem, not BAS.

Members on sea duty are *not* considered to be on temporary duty. Therefore, they do not receive a per diem, and the above meal collection rates are, in effect, debited from their BAS. However, as we discuss below, members on sea duty may qualify for Career Sea Pay.

FAMILY SEPARATION ALLOWANCE

FSA is payable to personnel with dependents who are separated from their dependents for reasons of duty. There are two types of FSA. FSA I is payable when transportation of dependents to a member's permanent duty station is not authorized at government expense, dependents do not live near the permanent duty station, and adequate quarters are not available at the station and adequate quarters have not been assigned to the member. In effect, FSA enables the member to acquire adequate housing reasonably near the permanent duty station. FSA II is payable because of an enforced family separation to personnel at any grade. The family separation can occur because the transportation of dependents is not an authorized government expense and the dependents do not live close by, or the member is on board ship or on temporary duty away from permanent station for more than 30 days. Members can receive both types of FSA at once. FSA II accounts for the vast majority of FSA in terms of dollar outlays and number of recipients. For instance, in 1995, 2,217 personnel received FSA I at a cost of $9.4 million, and 78,441 received FSA II at a cost of $70.6 million (Office of the Secretary of Defense, 1996, p. 777).

From January 1991 through December 1997, FSA II was paid at a rate of $75 per month. In January 1998 the rate increased to $100 per month. FSA I was paid at a rate equal to the basic allowance for quarters for a member without dependents at the same grade. Since June 1994, FSA II has been payable to personnel who are redeployed within 30 days of returning to their home port or permanent duty station. For instance, suppose a member was sent away from permanent station for more than 30 days of training prior to a deployment overseas, returned to permanent station for three weeks, and was then deployed for a three-month tour overseas. The member would receive FSA II continuously after the first 30 days of training.

HOSTILE FIRE/IMMINENT DANGER PAY

HFP is payable to members on duty in a foreign area who are

- Subjected to hostile fire or the explosion of a hostile mine,

- Near a hostile fire incident and in danger of being subject to hostile fire or mines,

- Killed (payable to their estate), injured, or wounded by hostile fire, mine, or action, or

- On official duty in a designated imminent danger area.[4]

HFP increased temporarily from $110 per month to $150 per month during the Gulf War, and the increase became permanent in FY1992. HFP is paid for service involving hostile fire or imminent danger in any part of the month. Hardship Duty Pay, as described below, was not authorized in places also designated for HFP. However, that changed as of November 1, 2001; Hardship Duty Pay and HFP can both be paid for the same locations.

---

[4]Data for our study cover deployments over the period from January 1992 to March 1999. During this period, some portion of the land, airspace, or sea area in the following countries was designated as an imminent danger area: Afghanistan, Albania, Algeria, Angola, Arabian Gulf area, Azerbaijan, Bahrain, Bosnia-Herzegovina, Burundi, Cambodia, Chad, Colombia, Croatia, Egypt, El Salvador, Georgia, Greece, Haiti, Iran, Iraq, Kuwait, Laos, Lebanon, Liberia, Macedonia, Montenegro, Mozambique, Oman, Pakistan, Peru, Qatar, Rwanda, Saudi Arabia, Serbia, Sierra Leone, Slovenia, Somalia, Sudan, Tajikistan, Turkey, United Arab Emirates, Vietnam, Yemen, Yugoslavia, Zaire (now the Democratic Republic of the Congo) (*Military Pay Policy and Procedures: Active Duty and Reserve Pay*, Chapter 10).

EXTENDING TOUR AT DESIGNATED OVERSEAS LOCATIONS

Some personnel may receive an award for extending their overseas tour of duty. The awards are designated for certain specialties and certain overseas locations and require that the member has completed a tour of duty at the location and must extend that tour for at least one more year. At the discretion of the Secretary of Defense, the member may receive either $80 per month or an annual bonus of up to $2,000. The bonus is payable in lump sum or installments. Alternatively, if permitted by the authority of the Secretary of Defense, the member may choose a "period of special rest and recuperative absence." Prior to October 1, 1997, only the $80 per month payment was offered.

COMBAT ZONE TAX EXCLUSION

This is formally referred to as the Income Tax Withholding Exclusion. As of the end of March 1996, the pay of active-duty personnel was no longer subject to federal and state income tax withholdings for any month in which the personnel served in a combat zone or hazardous duty area.[5] The tax exclusion may represent a prominent part of deployment-related pay for many personnel. It was fully in effect by April 1996 and so extended throughout our reenlistment study window, except for the beginning. Even though a withholding exclusion is not literally a pay, it is a pay in effect.

Members performing duty in combat zones qualified automatically for the income tax withholding exclusion during the months of duty there. In addition, members not in those areas but who received HFP and performed duties in direct support of members performing duties in combat zones, also qualified for the income tax withholding exclusion. Examples include the ground crew of aircraft flying missions into the combat zone or hazardous duty area, personnel

---

[5]As of April 1996, the withholding of taxes from commissioned officers was capped. Federal and state taxes were withheld only on officer income above the highest rate of pay of an enlisted member plus any hostile fire/imminent danger pay received during months for which the officer served in a combat zone or hazardous duty area. All pay of enlisted members and warrant officers earned in a combat zone is exempt from taxation.

engaged in transporting military supplies into the area, and airstrip personnel (e.g., air traffic controllers, meteorologists). Also included are support personnel and those who served in a combat zone or hazardous duty area but were hospitalized outside the area.[6]

If an enlisted member reenlisted while in a combat zone or hazardous duty area and received a reenlistment bonus, the full bonus amount—the initial lump sum payment plus subsequent installments—was not subject to federal and state income tax withholdings.

The list of combat zone/hazardous duty areas contains fewer countries than the list of hostile fire/imminent danger countries. However, many personnel who were deployed during 1992–1999 and received HFP probably also performed duty in a combat zone or hazardous duty area or performed supporting duty in a nearby area. These personnel would have received HFP and benefited from the state and federal income tax withholding exclusion during the months of this duty. In addition, personnel reenlisting and receiving a bonus would have been able to keep the full amount of the bonus.

To illustrate with a simple example, an E-4 with more than four years of service received $1,520 per month in basic pay as of July 1, 2001. Over three months, basic pay and HFP ($150 per month) totaled $5,010 before tax withholdings. Assuming a 20-percent withholding rate for federal and state taxes, this amount after taxes would be $4,008. The tax withholding exclusion therefore would have generated a $1,000 increase in income. Similarly, an E-5 with more than eight years of service had a three-month income from basic pay and HFP of $5,818, or $4,655 after a withholding of 20 percent. The implied increase in income exceeded $1,100. Finally, for an enlisted member reenlisting in a combat zone or hazardous duty area, a $5,000 bonus would not have been reduced to $4,000 by tax withholdings.

---

[6]From 1995 through 1999, the approximate span of reenlistment decisions covered in our study, combat zones included the Persian Gulf, Red Sea, Gulfs of Oman and Aden, portions of the Arabian Sea, Iraq, Kuwait, Saudi Arabia, Oman, Bahrain, Qatar, United Arab Emirates, and Vietnam. (Vietnam ceased to be a designated combat zone at the end of June 1996.) Hazardous duty areas included Boznia-Herzegovina, Croatia, and Macedonia.

Although our study focuses on enlisted members, officers too may benefit from the Combat Zone Tax Exclusion. Officers can exclude their pay up to the highest level of enlisted pay (E-9 with 26 years of service).

CAREER SEA PAY

Career Sea Pay is payable to a member in paygrade E-4 and above who is assigned to sea duty. Sea duty includes being permanently or temporarily assigned for duty to a ship, a ship-based staff, or ship-based aviation unit and serving on a ship whose primary mission is accomplished under way.

The amount of Career Sea Pay differs between officers and enlisted personnel and increases with paygrade and the cumulative amount of sea duty. For instance, an officer in grades O-1 to O-3 and with three years of sea duty receives $150 per month. An O-4 with 9 years of sea duty receives $220 per month, while an O-6 with 16 years of duty receives $340 per month. The pay schedule for warrant officers is somewhat more generous. A W-3 with over 12 years of sea duty receives $400 per month. Among enlisted members, an E-4 receives $50 per month with less than one year of sea duty and $150 per month with three years of duty. An E-5 with 7 years of sea duty receives $350 per month, an E-6 with 12 years of sea duty receives $380 per month, and an E-8 with 16 years of sea duty receives $500 per month.

CAREER SEA PAY PREMIUM

All officers and warrant officers who qualify for Career Sea Pay and who have served 36 consecutive months of sea duty qualify for the Career Sea Pay Premium. This is also true of enlisted members in paygrade E-4 under the same conditions. However, some E-4 enlisted members will not have accumulated 36 consecutive months of sea duty. The Career Sea Pay Premium is also payable to E-5 through E-9 members with at least three years but less than five years of sea duty with 36 consecutive months. Having qualified, a member is paid at the rate of $100 per month. The rate is the same for all who qualify.

HARDSHIP DUTY PAY

Hardship Duty Pay was implemented in February 1999 and replaced Foreign Duty Pay. Hardship Duty Pay covers two categories of duty: hardship locations and hardship missions. Hardship locations are designated in a list that includes a large number of countries and specific locations. During the months of 1999 in our data window, Hardship location pay was payable only to enlisted members, and the monthly rates of pay were $8 for E-1 and E-2, $9 for E-3, $13 for E-4, $16 for E-5, $20 for E-6, and $22.50 for E-7 through E-9. To qualify, members must spend at least 30 days in hardship locations. Hardship Duty Pay is paid only to personnel on the ground.

Hardship missions include locating and recovering the remains of U.S. servicemembers from remote, isolated areas in Laos, Cambodia, Vietnam, North Korea, and other designated assignments. Hardship mission assignments were paid at the rate of $150 per month for either full- or partial-month duty.

On November 1, 2001, the scope of Hardship Duty Pay was extended to allow personnel to receive HFP and Hardship Duty Pay for the same locations (Crawley, 2001). Hardship location pay is $50, $100, or $150 per month depending on the conditions of a location. When paid in conjunction with HFP, the rate is $100 per month, and the two pays together total $250 per month.

SUMMARY

We have presented information about seven deployment-related pays: BAS, FSA, HFP, award for extending an overseas tour, the federal and state income tax withholding exclusion, Career Sea Pay and Career Sea Pay Premium, and Hardship Duty Pay. Table A.1 summarizes these pays during 1995–1999, the reenlistment years of our study window.

Table A.1

Deployment-Related Pays, 1995–1999

Pay	Date of Change	Amount
Basic Allowance for Subsistence	Provisional as of the Gulf War, permanent on January 1, 1998	Made payable when deployed on temporary duty, with member receiving no less than when not deployed. (Members deployed on sea duty are not considered to be on temporary duty.)
		Members subsisted in kind became entitled to partial BAS. As of January 1, 2002 they will receive full BAS when deployed on temporary duty.
Family Separation Allowance II	To December 1997	$75/month
	From January 1998	$100/month
Hostile Fire/ Imminent Danger Pay	Throughout	$150/month
Overseas tour extension	To October 1997	$80/month
	From November 1997	$80/month, or up to $2,000 bonus, or special rest and recuperation.
Combat Zone Tax Exclusion	Effective March 1996 in combat zone and hazardous duty areas, and for personnel in direct support of activities in those areas and receiving HFP	Exclusion from federal and state income tax withholding. Equal to tax withheld from enlisted pay, plus tax on full amount of reenlistment bonus if reenlistment occurred when eligible for tax withholding exclusion.
Career Sea Pay	From October 1985 for officers, May 1988 for enlisted	Ranges from $50/month to $520/month depending on officer/enlisted, paygrade and years of sea duty.
Career Sea Pay Premium	From May 1988	$100/month
Hardship Duty Pay–mission	From February 1999	$150/month
Hardship Duty Pay–location	From February 1999	$8.00–$22.50/month for enlisted members only.

ACCURACY OF DEPLOYMENT MEASURES

ACCURACY OF EPISODE COUNT

Although we think the episode count is largely accurate, it may deviate from the true count for the reason that FSA and HFP are not meant to count episodes. Instead, they are meant to pay for the circumstances of being separated from dependents or having hostile duty at any time in a month. Here are possible examples of episode undercounts:

- An aircrew member makes two flights into hostile territory in a month but receives only a single HFP payment for the month.

- A member of a special-forces unit goes on hostile missions in two consecutive months, but because the months are consecutive, only a single episode is counted.

- A member with dependents is posted on an unaccompanied tour and during the tour is sent on a humanitarian mission in non-hostile territory. The member receives FSA throughout this entire period, and a single episode is inferred.

- A member may have also received a single catch-up payment for two or more episodes that were separated by periods without any deployment.

Data are not available to determine whether these examples represent rare or common occurrences, but the examples suggest that the use of FSA and HFP may result in some undercount of episodes. Still, the definition of "episode" need not go hand in hand with the number of particular missions. For instance, in the above example the air crew member made two separate flights into hostile airspace, but these might have been part of an overall operation lasting for weeks or months. The duration of the operation might be a more relevant measure of the episode than the number of flights into hostile airspace. If so, the fact that PERSTEMPO data might undercount the number of such flights would become irrelevant—the data would provide an accurate indicator that the aircrew member was involved in a hostile operation.

Another possible inaccuracy comes from the imputation of deployment to members without dependents. The imputation helps to identify nonhostile deployments. Hostile deployments, in contrast, are detected through HFP, which is receivable by members regardless of whether they have dependents. The imputation of nonhostile deployments can be inaccurate in certain cases, as the following examples illustrate:

- A unit is deployed but does not meet the criteria for imputing deployment to its members without dependents. In particular, fewer than 30 percent of unit members have dependents.

- A unit is deployed, but a member is ill or injured and either cannot deploy with the unit or has been sent back during deployment to recover. In this case, deployment is imputed to the member even though the member is not deployed while ill or injured.

- A unit is not deployed, but a member is attached to another, deploying unit that needs the member's specialty for the mission it has been given. In this case, the member deploys, but deployment is not imputed. The member's deployment is missed entirely unless it involves hostile duty.

It is possible to check the accuracy of the imputation algorithm by making use of data on personnel with dependents, for whom complete deployment data are available (insofar as deployment can be inferred from FSA and HFP). Thus, for members with dependents, we compared the episode count based on their actual FSA and HFP receipt with the episode count they would have had if handled as members without dependents. Again, the episode count of members

Table B.1

Weighted Kappa Values for Episode Counts

Episodes	Army	Navy	Air Force	Marine Corps
Total	0.89	0.85	0.98	0.95
Hostile	0.99	0.99	0.99	0.99

without dependents depends on HFP and an imputation based on unit deployment. The closeness of these counts is measured by the value of a weighted Kappa statistic, which measures the concordance between two categorical variables above that expected by chance, and the weighting recognizes that the agreement should occur along the diagonal. That is, if true episodes are equal to two, then ideally episodes based on imputation should equal two, etc. The maximum value of the weighted Kappa is one.

Table B.1 presents the weighted Kappa values for episode counts for our first- and second-term reenlistment samples by service. As seen, the values are all quite high, implying that episode counts for personnel without dependents are nearly as accurate as the counts for those with dependents. This is an important finding because most of our analysis uses episodes as the measure of deployments.

ACCURACY OF MONTH COUNT

The number of months in an episode of deployment is defined here as the string of months of in which FSA or HFP payments are received or a unit-deployed indicator is "on." There are several limitations of this approach. Its degree of resolution is the month, not the week or day, so there will be some inexactness about the actual length of the episode. Related to this, the receipt of payment does not have a one-to-one correspondence to the actual months in which the member was deployed. The first payment typically covers more than one month of deployment, and the last payment typically covers less than one month of deployment. The reason for this is that paperwork to document the member's eligibility for payment may not be turned in immediately, but instead may be batch-processed in a certain week of the month. Furthermore, in the case of FSA a member must be away for at least 30 days—a whole month—before becoming eligible to receive FSA, and as a result the member's first payment will typically cover a span of more than 30 days.

The PERSTEMPO data contain information about the receipt but not the amount of payment. Therefore, these data cannot be used to adjust the months of receipt of payment to reflect the number of months of deployment. To obtain information about the extent to which months of receipt undercount actual months of deployment, we made use of a separate data file containing data on the amount of FSA payments made to members in September 1997. These data are from the Joint Uniformed Military Pay System and were provided to us by the Defense Manpower Data Center. Because FSA payments are prorated to the number of days away per 30-day period, they can be used to infer the actual amount of time away. For instance, a member would receive $75 for a month in which he or she was away for at least 30 days, $150 for two months away, and $37.50 for 15 days away. In contrast, HFP payments are made when the member has hostile duty at any time in a month; the member is paid $150 whether the duty lasted the entire month or merely one hour.

Table B.2 tabulates the distribution of FSA payment amounts. The payments range from negative amounts, indicating the payback of

Table B.2

Distribution of FSA Payments in September 1997

Payment Amount	Fraction Receiving	Average Value	Value in Months
Negative	0.03	–$23	–0.31
$1–$74	0.22	$45	0.60
$75	0.62	$75	1.00
$76–$150	0.09	$111	1.47
$151–$225	0.02	$180	2.40
> $225	0.02	$314	4.19
Overall	1.00	$76	1.01
> $75	0.13	$154	2.05
> $75 but < $226	0.11	$123	1.64

past overpayments, to amounts in excess of $225, indicating a payment for three or more months away. A payment amount of $1 to $74 indicates a partial month away.

Utilizing certain assumptions, we can use the information in the table to make an estimate of the extent to which the months of receipt of FSA underestimates the actual months away. First, we assume that payments in excess of $75 can be used to estimate the average size of the first payment in an episode of deployment. This assumption comes from the notion that the first payment typically covers more than one month away. (Recall that FSA cannot be paid until the member has been away for at least 30 consecutive days.) Second, we assume that payments between $1 and $74 can be used to estimate the average size of the last payment in an episode of deployment. It is reasonable to suppose that most last payments cover only a fraction of a month. For instance, consider a deployment scheduled to be three months long. Only if the deployment began on the first day of a month and ended exactly as planned on the last day of the third month would the last FSA payment be $75. In other cases, the deployment would begin and end mid-month and therefore the final payment would be for part of a month.

We see from Table B.2 that 62 percent of the FSA payments were for $75 and therefore covered a full month away. In addition, 22 percent of the FSA payments were $1 to $74, with an average value of $45. The average value corresponds to $45/$75 = 0.60 of a month away. Also, 13 percent of the payments were in excess of $75. These payments had an average value of $154 or 2.05 months away. Two percent of the payments were in excess of $225 and therefore covered more than three months away.[1]

These payments could be viewed as statistical outliers and trimmed from the computation. If they were trimmed (see the last row of Table B.2), the average value of payments greater than $75 would be reduced from $154 to $123 and cover 1.64 months rather than 2.05 months. It is not clear whether they should be trimmed, but the argument in favor of trimming comes from their influence on the undercount estimate made below. By including the extreme values,

---

[1]These 2 percent are part of the 13 percent of payments greater than $75. They account for 2/13, or about 15 percent, of the payments greater than $75.

all members with a payment greater than \$75 would be assumed to have an average undercount of 1.05 months, whereas for five out of six members the undercount would be no more than 0.64 months.

Using the assumptions and leaving the data untrimmed, the average first month payment covers 2.05 months and the average last month payment covers 0.60 months. The use of months of receipt of FSA therefore undercounts the beginning of an episode by $2.05 - 1.00 = 1.05$ months on average, and overcounts the ending of an episode by $1.00 - 0.60 = 0.40$ months. Therefore, there is a net undercount of $1.05 - 0.40 = 0.65$ months per episode on average or about 2.5 weeks per episode. If the data are trimmed to exclude payments above \$225, the beginning of the episode is undercounted by $1.64 - 1.00 = 0.64$ months and the end is, as before, overcounted by 0.40 months. The net undercount is now $0.64 - 0.40 = 0.24$ months per episode, or about one week.

Because members may have more than one episode of deployment, we present Table B.3 to show how these undercounts cumulate as the number of episodes increases.

As a final step, we put these estimates into perspective by referring to Table B.2, which shows that most members who are deployed have only one episode of deployment. Also, we have separately tabulated that the average length of a hostile episode for a member who had only one hostile episode is 4.6 months for the Army, 3.0 months for the Navy, 3.8 months for the Air Force, and 2.7 months for the Marine Corps. Using the trimmed estimate for the undercount of months, each of these figures would be increased by 0.24 months.

Table B.3

Estimate of Undercount of Months of Deployment per Episode

	Undercount of Months	
Number of Episodes	Raw data	Trimmed data[a]
1	0.65	0.24
2	1.30	0.48
3	1.95	0.72
4	2.60	0.96

[a]First month payment is assumed to be \$76 to \$225.

MEANS AND STANDARD DEVIATIONS

This appendix contains the means and standard deviations by service for the variables used in the empirical analysis. Table C.1 is for first-term members, and Table C.2 is for second-term members. (For complete definitions of the variables used in this appendix, please see Appendix E.)

Table C.1

Sample Means and Standard Deviation: First Term

Variable	Army		Navy		Air Force		Marine Corps	
	Mean	SD	Mean	SD	Mean	SD	Mean	SD
N1H0	0.2055	0.4041	0.1307	0.3371	0.1282	0.3343	0.2725	0.4453
N2H0	0.0741	0.2619	0.0444	0.2060	0.0334	0.1798	0.1269	0.3329
N3H0	0.0135	0.1152	0.0304	0.1716	0.0092	0.0957	0.0534	0.2249
N0H1	0.1333	0.3399	0.0977	0.2970	0.1501	0.3571	0.0592	0.2361
N1H1	0.0535	0.2250	0.0659	0.2481	0.0428	0.2025	0.0473	0.2123
N2H1	0.0140	0.1176	0.0379	0.1908	0.0106	0.1024	0.0193	0.1377
N3H1	0.0028	0.0532	0.0225	0.1483	0.0025	0.0502	0.0058	0.0760
N0H2	0.0309	0.1732	0.0237	0.1520	0.0473	0.2123	0.0139	0.1170
N1H2	0.0105	0.1018	0.0181	0.1334	0.0124	0.1106	0.0086	0.0924
N2H2	0.0022	0.0464	0.0109	0.1039	0.0032	0.0567	0.0012	0.0351
N3H2	0.0004	0.0211	0.0067	0.0815	0.0009	0.0293	0.0014	0.0375
N0H3	0.0066	0.0808	0.0046	0.0679	0.0350	0.1837	0.0021	0.0459
N1H3	0.0017	0.0413	0.0022	0.0467	0.0070	0.0834	0.0007	0.0265
N2H3	0.0003	0.0176	0.0010	0.0316	0.0015	0.0393	0.0000	0.0000
N3H3	0.0000	0.0000	0.0005	0.0213	0.0004	0.0193	0.0000	0.0000
AFQTI_II	0.2891	0.4533	0.2124	0.4090	0.4932	0.5000	0.3674	0.4822

Table C.1—continued

Variable	Army Mean	Army SD	Navy Mean	Navy SD	Air Force Mean	Air Force SD	Marine Corps Mean	Marine Corps SD
AFQTIIIA	0.2872	0.4524	0.2067	0.4050	0.3100	0.4625	0.3119	0.4633
AFQTIV	0.0367	0.1879	0.1307	0.3371	0.0023	0.0476	0.0026	0.0513
AFQTMISS	0.0191	0.1368	0.0555	0.2289	0.0141	0.1180	0.0097	0.0979
GED	0.0340	0.1811	0.0330	0.1786	0.0004	0.0198	0.0369	0.1886
NHSG	0.0036	0.0601	0.0220	0.1467	0.0000	0.0000	0.0005	0.0230
SPSS	0.0263	0.1601	0.0265	0.1607	0.9464	0.2253	0.0178	0.1321
FEMALE	0.1430	0.3501	0.1347	0.3414	0.1777	0.3822	0.0714	0.2575
BLACK	0.3684	0.4824	0.3311	0.4706	0.1629	0.3693	0.2449	0.4301
HISPANIC	0.0578	0.2334	0.0921	0.2892	0.0357	0.1855	0.1072	0.3094
DEPEND	0.8249	0.3801	0.8055	0.3959	0.7997	0.4002	0.8261	0.3790
PMOS_I1	0.0796	0.2707	0.0790	0.2698	0.1177	0.3222	0.0545	0.2270
PMOS_I2	0.0893	0.2851	0.0833	0.2763	0.0759	0.2648	0.0777	0.2677
PMOS_I3	0.0920	0.2890	0.1479	0.3550	0.0898	0.2859	0.0000	0.0000
PMOS_I4	0.0246	0.1550	0.0142	0.1182	0.0391	0.1938	0.0276	0.1638
PMOS_I5	0.1859	0.3890	0.1106	0.3137	0.2312	0.4216	0.2672	0.4426
PMOS_I6	0.1782	0.3827	0.3064	0.4610	0.2558	0.4363	0.1799	0.3841
PMOS_I7	0.0221	0.1471	0.0589	0.2354	0.0499	0.2176	0.0294	0.1688
PMOS_I8	0.1309	0.3373	0.0954	0.2938	0.0667	0.2496	0.1923	0.3942
UNEPLY_A	5.9909	0.8146	5.7761	0.6804	5.7273	0.6506	5.9323	0.7204
UNEPLY_R	4.9295	0.4498	4.8365	0.4688	4.9015	0.4705	4.8243	0.4302
ETS97	0.3423	0.4745	0.2533	0.4349	0.2616	0.4395	0.2449	0.4301
ETS98	0.2551	0.4359	0.2683	0.4431	0.2547	0.4357	0.3488	0.4766
ETS99	0.1845	0.3879	0.2754	0.4467	0.2271	0.4189	0.2540	0.4354

Table C.2

Sample Means and Standard Deviation: Second Term

Variable	Army Mean	Army SD	Navy Mean	Navy SD	Air Force Mean	Air Force SD	Marine Corps Mean	Marine Corps SD
N1H0	0.2055	0.4041	0.1307	0.3371	0.1282	0.3343	0.2725	0.4453
N2H0	0.0741	0.2619	0.0444	0.2060	0.0334	0.1798	0.1269	0.3329
N3H0	0.0135	0.1152	0.0304	0.1716	0.0092	0.0957	0.0534	0.2249
N0H1	0.1333	0.3399	0.0977	0.2970	0.1501	0.3571	0.0592	0.2361
N1H1	0.0535	0.2250	0.0659	0.2481	0.0428	0.2025	0.0473	0.2123
N2H1	0.0140	0.1176	0.0379	0.1908	0.0106	0.1024	0.0193	0.1377

Table C.2—continued

Variable	Army Mean	Army SD	Navy Mean	Navy SD	Air Force Mean	Air Force SD	Marine Corps Mean	Marine Corps SD
N3H1	0.0028	0.0532	0.0225	0.1483	0.0025	0.0502	0.0058	0.0760
N0H2	0.0309	0.1732	0.0237	0.1520	0.0473	0.2123	0.0139	0.1170
N1H2	0.0105	0.1018	0.0181	0.1334	0.0124	0.1106	0.0086	0.0924
N2H2	0.0022	0.0464	0.0109	0.1039	0.0032	0.0567	0.0012	0.0351
N3H2	0.0004	0.0211	0.0067	0.0815	0.0009	0.0293	0.0014	0.0375
N0H3	0.0066	0.0808	0.0046	0.0679	0.0350	0.1837	0.0021	0.0459
N1H3	0.0017	0.0413	0.0022	0.0467	0.0070	0.0834	0.0007	0.0265
N2H3	0.0003	0.0176	0.0010	0.0316	0.0015	0.0393	0.0000	0.0000
N3H3	0.0000	0.0000	0.0005	0.0213	0.0004	0.0193	0.0000	0.0000
AFQTI_II	0.2891	0.4533	0.2124	0.4090	0.4932	0.5000	0.3674	0.4822
AFQTIIIA	0.2872	0.4524	0.2067	0.4050	0.3100	0.4625	0.3119	0.4633
AFQTIV	0.0367	0.1879	0.1307	0.3371	0.0023	0.0476	0.0026	0.0513
AFQTMISS	0.0191	0.1368	0.0555	0.2289	0.0141	0.1180	0.0097	0.0979
GED	0.0340	0.1811	0.0330	0.1786	0.0004	0.0198	0.0369	0.1886
NHSG	0.0036	0.0601	0.0220	0.1467	0.0000	0.0000	0.0005	0.0230
SPSS	0.0263	0.1601	0.0265	0.1607	0.9464	0.2253	0.0178	0.1321
FEMALE	0.1430	0.3501	0.1347	0.3414	0.1777	0.3822	0.0714	0.2575
BLACK	0.3684	0.4824	0.3311	0.4706	0.1629	0.3693	0.2449	0.4301
HISPANIC	0.0578	0.2334	0.0921	0.2892	0.0357	0.1855	0.1072	0.3094
DEPEND	0.8249	0.3801	0.8055	0.3959	0.7997	0.4002	0.8261	0.3790
PMOS_I1	0.0796	0.2707	0.0790	0.2698	0.1177	0.3222	0.0545	0.2270
PMOS_I2	0.0893	0.2851	0.0833	0.2763	0.0759	0.2648	0.0777	0.2677
PMOS_I3	0.0920	0.2890	0.1479	0.3550	0.0898	0.2859	0.0000	0.0000
PMOS_I4	0.0246	0.1550	0.0142	0.1182	0.0391	0.1938	0.0276	0.1638
PMOS_I5	0.1859	0.3890	0.1106	0.3137	0.2312	0.4216	0.2672	0.4426
PMOS_I6	0.1782	0.3827	0.3064	0.4610	0.2558	0.4363	0.1799	0.3841
PMOS_I7	0.0221	0.1471	0.0589	0.2354	0.0499	0.2176	0.0294	0.1688
PMOS_I8	0.1309	0.3373	0.0954	0.2938	0.0667	0.2496	0.1923	0.3942
UNEPLY_A	5.9909	0.8146	5.7761	0.6804	5.7273	0.6506	5.9323	0.7204
UNEPLY_R	4.9295	0.4498	4.8365	0.4688	4.9015	0.4705	4.8243	0.4302
ETS97	0.3423	0.4745	0.2533	0.4349	0.2616	0.4395	0.2449	0.4301
ETS98	0.2551	0.4359	0.2683	0.4431	0.2547	0.4357	0.3488	0.4766
ETS99	0.1845	0.3879	0.2754	0.4467	0.2271	0.4189	0.2540	0.4354

REGRESSION RESULTS

Tables D.1–D.8 contain regression results by service for the following models:

- Main-effect probit model of reenlistment: first term.

- Main-effect probit model of reenlistment: second term.

- Full-interaction probit model of reenlistment: first term.

- Full-interaction probit model of reenlistment: second term.

- Main-effect probit model of reenlistment: first-term members with no dependents at the time of their reenlistment decision.

- Main-effect probit model of reenlistment: first-term members with dependents at the time of their reenlistment decision.

- Tobit/probit model of time to promotion to E-5 and reenlistment: first term.

- Tobit/probit model of time to promotion to E-5 and reenlistment: second term.

(For complete definitions of the variables used in this appendix, please see Appendix E.)

Table D.1

Main-Effect Probit Model of Reenlistment: First Term

Variable	Army	Navy	Air Force	Marine Corps
Const2	−3.2649 ***	−3.7470 ***	0.6997 ***	−1.4717 ***
	(0.1699)	(0.1784)	(0.1641)	(0.0188)
N1	0.2659 ***	0.0676 ***	0.3048 ***	0.0431 ***
	(0.0113)	(0.0139)	(0.0137)	(0.0124)
N2	0.4282 ***	0.0617 ***	0.4454 ***	0.0977 ***
	(0.0201)	(0.0150)	(0.0311)	(0.0156)
N3	0.5547 ***	0.2168 ***	0.3772 ***	0.2143 ***
	(0.0437)	(0.0159)	(0.0631)	(0.0236)
H1	0.1709 ***	−0.0728 ***	0.0292 **	0.0426 ***
	(0.0123)	(0.0124)	(0.0118)	(0.0134)
H2	0.1742 ***	−0.0170	−0.0094	0.0156
	(0.0243)	(0.0157)	(0.0182)	(0.0229)
H3	0.2412 ***	0.1987 ***	0.0396 *	0.0429
	(0.0544)	(0.0397)	(0.0235)	(0.0629)
AFQTI_II	−0.0420 ***	−0.0018	−0.1217 ***	0.0853 ***
	(0.0149)	(0.0137)	(0.0140)	(0.0135)
AFQTIIIA	0.0098	−0.0359 **	−0.0650 ***	0.0614 ***
	(0.0149)	(0.0143)	(0.0147)	(0.0138)
AFQTIV	−0.0342	0.2748 ***	0.0601	0.0011
	(0.0498)	(0.1059)	(0.1330)	(0.1159)
AFQTMISS	0.0328	0.1785 ***	−0.0144	−0.0025
	(0.0277)	(0.0245)	(0.0278)	(0.0236)
GED	0.0796 **	0.0681 **	−0.0869	−0.0208
	(0.0340)	(0.0317)	(0.1132)	(0.0294)
NHSG	−0.1006	0.1148 **	0.7512	0.0179
	(0.0870)	(0.0572)	(0.5129)	(0.1863)
SPSS	−0.1193 ***	0.0462	−0.1482 ***	−0.0276
	(0.0244)	(0.0400)	(0.0114)	(0.0460)
FEMALE	0.1312 ***	−0.1893 ***	0.0093	0.0791 ***
	(0.0139)	(0.0157)	(0.0122)	(0.0246)
BLACK	0.4282 ***	0.4567 ***	0.3967 ***	0.3717 ***
	(0.0127)	(0.0142)	(0.0142)	(0.0149)
HISPANIC	0.2499 ***	0.0886 ***	0.0589 **	0.1281 ***
	(0.0198)	(0.0171)	(0.0231)	(0.0162)
DEPEND	0.2327 ***	0.4153 ***	0.2040 ***	0.3436 ***
	(0.0101)	(0.0104)	(0.0094)	(0.0109)

Table D.1—continued

Variable	Army	Navy	Air Force	Marine Corps
PMOS_I1	−0.0104	0.4956 ***	0.3079 ***	0.3947 ***
	(0.0191)	(0.0235)	(0.0198)	(0.0234)
PMOS_I2	0.0198	0.4565 ***	0.3174 ***	0.2232 ***
	(0.0196)	(0.0222)	(0.0227)	(0.0200)
PMOS_I3	0.1654 ***	0.3985 ***	0.3326 ***	
	(0.0191)	(0.0249)	(0.0211)	
PMOS_I4	0.1754 ***	0.5163 ***	0.0361	0.3576 ***
	(0.0303)	(0.0470)	(0.0266)	(0.0346)
PMOS_I5	0.2011 ***	0.3151 ***	0.4115 ***	0.4376 ***
	(0.0177)	(0.0226)	(0.0179)	(0.0167)
PMOS_I6	−0.0104	0.1237 ***	0.3248 ***	0.3057 ***
	(0.0182)	(0.0193)	(0.0167)	(0.0157)
PMOS_I7	−0.0035	−0.0102	0.1935 ***	0.2060 ***
	(0.0286)	(0.0268)	(0.0248)	(0.0302)
PMOS_I8	0.0563 ***	0.2466 ***	0.1743 ***	0.1876 ***
	(0.0197)	(0.0270)	(0.0215)	(0.0162)
UNEPLY_A	−0.2149 ***	0.0078	−0.5134 ***	
	(0.0082)	(0.0105)	(0.0075)	
UNEPLY_R	0.7480 ***	0.4854 ***	0.4971 ***	
	(0.0299)	(0.0310)	(0.0291)	
ETS97	0.4002 ***	0.1423 ***	−0.0185	0.0363 **
	(0.0167)	(0.0183)	(0.0166)	(0.0146)
ETS98	0.6020 ***	0.5105 ***	−0.1121 ***	0.0608 ***
	(0.0300)	(0.0316)	(0.0294)	(0.0148)
ETS99	0.6424 ***	0.5684 ***	−0.3789 ***	0.0572 ***
	(0.0380)	(0.0399)	(0.0367)	(0.0147)

NOTE: Standard errors in parentheses. *** = significant at 0.01, ** = significant at 0.05, * = significant at 0.10.

Table D.2

Main-Effect Probit Model of Reenlistment: Second Term

Variable	Army	Navy	Air Force	Marine Corps
Const2	−1.5824 ***	−1.5888 ***	−0.2478	−0.1953 **
	(0.2607)	(0.3095)	(0.2029)	(0.0772)
N1	0.2626 ***	0.3022 ***	0.1938 ***	0.2766 ***
	(0.0175)	(0.0224)	(0.0148)	(0.0402)
N2	0.2879 ***	0.3296 ***	0.1726 ***	0.5082 ***
	(0.0270)	(0.0316)	(0.0270)	(0.0537)
N3	0.3396 ***	0.6113 ***	0.2507 ***	0.8119 ***
	(0.0593)	(0.0402)	(0.0517)	(0.0833)
H1	0.2283 ***	0.1636 ***	0.1134 ***	0.2981 ***
	(0.0192)	(0.0222)	(0.0145)	(0.0530)
H2	0.3133 ***	0.4758 ***	0.1727 ***	0.5275 ***
	(0.0370)	(0.0392)	(0.0241)	(0.1107)
H3	0.1282	0.6317 ***	0.1804 ***	0.4269
	(0.0814)	(0.1021)	(0.0290)	(0.3686)
AFQTI_II	0.0311	0.1202 ***	0.0877 ***	0.1079 **
	(0.0202)	(0.0256)	(0.0163)	(0.0460)
AFQTIIIA	0.0369 *	0.0298	0.0713 ***	0.1234 ***
	(0.0193)	(0.0245)	(0.0169)	(0.0450)
AFQTIV	−0.1657 ***	−0.1128 ***	−0.3079 ***	−0.0384
	(0.0417)	(0.0279)	(0.1156)	(0.3922)
AFQTMISS	0.2454 ***	0.2590 ***	0.2218 ***	0.3024 *
	(0.0564)	(0.0409)	(0.0505)	(0.1756)
GED	−0.0561	−0.1571 ***	0.1923	−0.0964
	(0.0425)	(0.0488)	(0.2838)	(0.0896)
NHSG	−0.1351	−0.2173 ***	0.7512	−0.9308
	(0.1259)	(0.0592)	(0.0000)	(0.7936)
SPSS	0.2455 ***	0.1393 **	0.1174 ***	−0.1158
	(0.0481)	(0.0552)	(0.0253)	(0.1306)
FEMALE	0.1129 ***	−0.1438 ***	−0.1064 ***	−0.0539
	(0.0236)	(0.0263)	(0.0158)	(0.0700)
BLACK	0.2994 ***	0.0144	0.1492 ***	0.2180 ***
	(0.0175)	(0.0202)	(0.0160)	(0.0437)
HISPANIC	0.1355 ***	0.0286	0.1161 ***	0.1081 *
	(0.0327)	(0.0309)	(0.0310)	(0.0578)
DEPEND	0.2371 ***	0.1527 ***	0.1564 ***	0.0763 *
	(0.0201)	(0.0219)	(0.0142)	(0.0462)

Table D.2—continued

Variable	Army	Navy	Air Force	Marine Corps
PMOS_I1	−0.0208	0.4409 ***	0.0137	−0.0624
	(0.0321)	(0.0431)	(0.0269)	(0.0881)
PMOS_I2	0.1101 ***	0.2214 ***	−0.0777 ***	0.1215
	(0.0303)	(0.0406)	(0.0295)	(0.0764)
PMOS_I3	0.1837 ***	0.3995 ***	0.1264 ***	
	(0.0314)	(0.0362)	(0.0291)	
PMOS_I4	0.3607 ***	0.2626 ***	−0.0118	0.2258 **
	(0.0509)	(0.0777)	(0.0354)	(0.1134)
PMOS_I5	0.2428 ***	0.3590 ***	0.1727 ***	0.1196 **
	(0.0264)	(0.0379)	(0.0247)	(0.0574)
PMOS_I6	0.0295	0.0224	0.1390 ***	0.0155
	(0.0246)	(0.0311)	(0.0238)	(0.0585)
PMOS_I7	0.1765 ***	0.1770 ***	0.1005 ***	0.1430
	(0.0524)	(0.0446)	(0.0331)	(0.1101)
PMOS_I8	−0.0040	−0.1220 ***	0.1736 ***	0.0840
	(0.0270)	(0.0389)	(0.0308)	(0.0587)
UNEPLY_A	0.1488 ***	0.1364 ***	−0.0670 ***	
	(0.0115)	(0.0143)	(0.0094)	
UNEPLY_R	−0.0407	0.0820	0.0768 **	
	(0.0445)	(0.0530)	(0.0343)	
ETS97	0.5416 ***	0.0548 *	−0.0048	0.0701
	(0.0249)	(0.0331)	(0.0199)	(0.0574)
ETS98	0.3479 ***	0.0534	0.0727 **	−0.0127
	(0.0446)	(0.0548)	(0.0342)	(0.0536)
ETS99	0.2629 ***	0.1196 *	0.0565	−0.4736 ***
	(0.0554)	(0.0666)	(0.0424)	(0.0564)

NOTE: Standard errors in parentheses. *** = significant at 0.01, ** = significant at 0.05, * = significant at 0.10.

Table D.3

Full-Interaction Probit Model of Reenlishtment: First Term

Variable	Army	Navy	Air Force	Marine Corps
N1H0	0.2775 ***	0.1556 ***	0.3456 ***	0.0426 ***
	(0.0131)	(0.0216)	(0.0166)	(0.0145)
N2H0	0.4297 ***	0.1364 ***	0.4994 ***	0.0971 ***
	(0.0222)	(0.0237)	(0.0378)	(0.0175)
N3H0	0.5554 ***	0.3176 ***	0.3772 ***	0.2129 ***
	(0.0479)	(0.0222)	(0.0734)	(0.0254)
N0H1	0.1820 ***	0.0483 **	0.0534 ***	0.0390 **
	(0.0149)	(0.0208)	(0.0130)	(0.0195)
N1H1	0.4214 ***	0.0189	0.2654 ***	0.0811 ***
	(0.0228)	(0.0198)	(0.0272)	(0.0217)
N2H1	0.5881 ***	0.0415 **	0.3481 ***	0.1547 ***
	(0.0501)	(0.0209)	(0.0664)	(0.0323)
N3H1	0.7608 ***	0.1273 ***	0.4086 ***	0.2854 ***
	(0.1141)	(0.0245)	(0.1526)	(0.0636)
N0H2	0.1949 ***	0.0756 ***	0.0084	0.0301
	(0.0280)	(0.0262)	(0.0199)	(0.0291)
N1H2	0.3460 ***	0.0890 ***	0.2458 ***	0.0583
	(0.0536)	(0.0260)	(0.0469)	(0.0411)
N2H2	0.7919 ***	0.0492 *	0.3604 ***	0.0233
	(0.1256)	(0.0294)	(0.1096)	(0.0816)
N3H2	0.7350 **	0.2548 ***	0.4923 **	0.0165
	(0.3418)	(0.0363)	(0.2432)	(0.2119)
N0H3	0.2251 ***	0.3345 ***	0.0498 **	−0.0390
	(0.0624)	(0.0614)	(0.0249)	(0.0744)
N1H3	0.6413 ***	0.3131 ***	0.3063 ***	0.3174 **
	(0.1267)	(0.0682)	(0.0747)	(0.1266)
N2H3	0.5541 **	0.2047 **	0.5522 ***	0.2448
	(0.2467)	(0.0898)	(0.1777)	(0.3472)
N3H3	0.2607	0.2426	0.3496	
	(0.6023)	(0.1543)	(0.3970)	

NOTE: The regression also contains all the other explanatory variables in Table D.1. Standard errors in parentheses. *** = significant at 0.01, ** = significant at 0.05, * = significant at 0.10.

Table D.4

Full-Interaction Probit Model of Reenlistment: Second Term

Variable	Army	Navy	Air Force	Marine Corps
N1H0	0.2822 ***	0.3835 ***	0.2083 ***	0.2757 ***
	(0.0202)	(0.0273)	(0.0179)	(0.0437)
N2H0	0.3068 ***	0.4408 ***	0.1711 ***	0.4935 ***
	(0.0301)	(0.0434)	(0.0323)	(0.0572)
N3H0	0.3627 ***	0.6760 ***	0.2010 ***	0.8585 ***
	(0.0658)	(0.0544)	(0.0603)	(0.0897)
N0H1	0.2530 ***	0.2684 ***	0.1257 ***	0.2546 ***
	(0.0237)	(0.0306)	(0.0168)	(0.0763)
N1H1	0.4691 ***	0.4042 ***	0.2621 ***	0.6152 ***
	(0.0351)	(0.0367)	(0.0293)	(0.0868)
N2H1	0.5064 ***	0.4611 ***	0.3155 ***	0.9065 ***
	(0.0654)	(0.0479)	(0.0577)	(0.1383)
N3H1	0.4279 ***	0.8013 ***	0.4047 ***	0.9273 ***
	(0.1458)	(0.0643)	(0.1177)	(0.2609)
N0H2	0.3420 ***	0.6539 ***	0.1785 ***	0.7379 ***
	(0.0439)	(0.0595)	(0.0277)	(0.1562)
N1H2	0.5414 ***	0.7200 ***	0.3512 ***	0.5889 ***
	(0.0760)	(0.0703)	(0.0535)	(0.1839)
N2H2	0.4190 ***	0.7051 ***	0.2139 **	1.1714
	(0.1602)	(0.0859)	(0.1014)	(0.7195)
N3H2	1.2338 ***	0.9580 ***	1.1520 ***	0.4279
	(0.4295)	(0.1193)	(0.2664)	(0.4420)
N0H3	0.2286 **	0.8589 ***	0.1605 ***	0.4238
	(0.0942)	(0.1400)	(0.0320)	(0.4029)
N1H3	0.1542	0.8659 ***	0.4611 ***	0.7237
	(0.1856)	(0.1994)	(0.0731)	(0.9090)
N2H3	−0.1787	0.5501 *	0.5374 ***	0.1657 ***
	(0.4307)	(0.2961)	(0.1546)	(0.0000)
N3H3	0.2607	0.5205	0.3197	1.0144 ***
	(0.0000)	(0.4895)	(0.3084)	(0.0000)

NOTE: The regression also contains all the other explanatory variables in Table D.2. Standard errors in parentheses. *** = significant at 0.01, ** = significant at 0.05, * = significant at 0.10.

Table D.5

Main-Effect Probit Model of Reenlistment: First Term with No Dependents

Variable	Army	Navy	Air Force	Marine Corps
Const2	-4.1180 ***	-3.9443 ***	0.5958 **	-1.4069 ***
	(0.2631)	(0.2601)	(0.2542)	(0.0278)
N1	0.1641 ***	-0.0540 **	0.1832 ***	-0.0198
	(0.0177)	(0.0215)	(0.0244)	(0.0205)
N2	0.3181 ***	-0.0840 ***	0.1617 **	-0.0457 *
	(0.0365)	(0.0218)	(0.0762)	(0.0275)
N3	0.3498 ***	0.0461 **	0.1045	-0.0165
	(0.0742)	(0.0217)	(0.1609)	(0.0554)
H1	0.1519 ***	-0.0985 ***	0.0328 *	0.0120
	(0.0183)	(0.0181)	(0.0176)	(0.0202)
H2	0.0883 **	-0.0810 ***	-0.0196	-0.0827 **
	(0.0351)	(0.0221)	(0.0253)	(0.0324)
H3	0.1083	0.2072 ***	0.0075	-0.1798 **
	(0.0785)	(0.0526)	(0.0312)	(0.0820)
AFQTI_II	-0.0483 **	-0.0270	-0.1471 ***	0.0432 **
	(0.0236)	(0.0199)	(0.0216)	(0.0207)
AFQTIIIA	0.0237	-0.0520 **	-0.0793 ***	0.0249
	(0.0238)	(0.0212)	(0.0226)	(0.0216)
AFQTIV	0.1108	0.2497	0.1601	-0.3945 *
	(0.0828)	(0.1593)	(0.2099)	(0.2162)
AFQTMISS	0.0642	0.1040 ***	-0.0454	-0.0099
	(0.0422)	(0.0362)	(0.0432)	(0.0360)
GED	0.1851 ***	-0.0041	-0.0768	-0.0091
	(0.0611)	(0.0518)	(0.2030)	(0.0518)
NHSG	-0.0369	0.1825 **	0.8453	0.0889
	(0.1273)	(0.0873)	(0.8089)	(0.2943)
SPSS	-0.0803 **	0.0596	-0.1764 ***	-0.0092
	(0.0396)	(0.0583)	(0.0174)	(0.0713)
FEMALE	0.2511 ***	0.1037 ***	0.1431 ***	0.3224 ***
	(0.0234)	(0.0250)	(0.0198)	(0.0460)
BLACK	0.4674 ***	0.5365 ***	0.4234 ***	0.4690 ***
	(0.0200)	(0.0214)	(0.0211)	(0.0235)
HISPANIC	0.1917 ***	0.0715 ***	-0.0296	0.1064 ***
	(0.0318)	(0.0257)	(0.0365)	(0.0266)
PMOS_I1	-0.0037	0.5081 ***	0.2828 ***	0.3727 ***
	(0.0282)	(0.0335)	(0.0298)	(0.0367)

Table D.5—continued

Variable	Army	Navy	Air Force	Marine Corps
PMOS_I2	0.0081	0.4365 ***	0.3233 ***	0.1728 ***
	(0.0282)	(0.0314)	(0.0340)	(0.0303)
PMOS_I3	0.1305 ***	0.3379 ***	0.2378 ***	
	(0.0296)	(0.0379)	(0.0329)	
PMOS_I4	0.1737 ***	0.5594 ***	0.0036	0.4131 ***
	(0.0447)	(0.0654)	(0.0412)	(0.0518)
PMOS_I5	0.1559 ***	0.3143 ***	0.3852 ***	0.4352 ***
	(0.0265)	(0.0331)	(0.0272)	(0.0261)
PMOS_I6	0.0042	0.1572 ***	0.2827 ***	0.3147 ***
	(0.0278)	(0.0278)	(0.0253)	(0.0242)
PMOS_I7	0.0809 *	0.0248	0.2008 ***	0.2103 ***
	(0.0453)	(0.0402)	(0.0391)	(0.0479)
PMOS_I8	0.0990 ***	0.2992 ***	0.1531 ***	0.1728 ***
	(0.0303)	(0.0392)	(0.0332)	(0.0257)
UNEPLY_A	−0.4023 ***	−0.0191	−0.7241 ***	
	(0.0137)	(0.0159)	(0.0118)	
UNEPLY_R	1.1509 ***	0.5700 ***	0.8130 ***	
	(0.0466)	(0.0452)	(0.0452)	
ETS97	0.5240 ***	0.1860 ***	−0.0170	0.0016
	(0.0263)	(0.0268)	(0.0261)	(0.0227)
ETS98	0.8018 ***	0.5690 ***	−0.0958 **	0.0568 **
	(0.0467)	(0.0463)	(0.0459)	(0.0228)
ETS99	0.8843 ***	0.6609 ***	−0.4313 ***	0.0872 ***
	(0.0592)	(0.0583)	(0.0569)	(0.0230)

NOTE: Standard errors in parentheses. *** = significant at 0.01, ** = significant at 0.05, * = significant at 0.10.

Table D.6

Main-Effect Probit Model of Reenlistment: First Term with Dependents

Variable	Army	Navy	Air Force	Marine Corps
Const2	−2.2249 ***	−3.0886 ***	1.1558 ***	−1.1794 ***
	(0.2244)	(0.2465)	(0.2164)	(0.0254)
N1	0.3343 ***	0.1415 ***	0.3525 ***	0.0992 ***
	(0.0149)	(0.0183)	(0.0166)	(0.0158)
N2	0.4812 ***	0.1698 ***	0.4932 ***	0.1786 ***
	(0.0241)	(0.0209)	(0.0343)	(0.0193)
N3	0.6703 ***	0.3895 ***	0.4211 ***	0.2916 ***
	(0.0541)	(0.0239)	(0.0691)	(0.0266)
H1	0.1785 ***	−0.0505 ***	0.0209	0.0645 ***
	(0.0167)	(0.0171)	(0.0160)	(0.0180)
H2	0.2325 ***	0.0576 **	−0.0044	0.1136 ***
	(0.0338)	(0.0226)	(0.0263)	(0.0324)
H3	0.3450 ***	0.1605 ***	0.0855 **	0.3664 ***
	(0.0752)	(0.0611)	(0.0359)	(0.1011)
AFQTI_II	−0.0314	0.0194	−0.1057 ***	0.1194 ***
	(0.0194)	(0.0190)	(0.0185)	(0.0179)
AFQTIIIA	0.0035	−0.0241	−0.0520 ***	0.0892 ***
	(0.0192)	(0.0196)	(0.0195)	(0.0179)
AFQTIV	−0.1079 *	0.2902 **	−0.0069	0.1846
	(0.0629)	(0.1447)	(0.1759)	(0.1385)
AFQTMISS	0.0050	0.2374 ***	0.0109	0.0002
	(0.0371)	(0.0334)	(0.0367)	(0.0315)
GED	0.0349	0.1038 ***	−0.0915	−0.0301
	(0.0413)	(0.0400)	(0.1379)	(0.0357)
NHSG	−0.1559	0.0714	0.7204	−0.0622
	(0.1208)	(0.0762)	(0.6989)	(0.2428)
SPSS	−0.1531 ***	0.0120	−0.1293 ***	−0.0545
	(0.0310)	(0.0554)	(0.0152)	(0.0612)
FEMALE	0.0756 ***	−0.3413 ***	−0.0689 ***	0.0147
	(0.0174)	(0.0212)	(0.0157)	(0.0298)
BLACK	0.4031 ***	0.3966 ***	0.3626 ***	0.3083 ***
	(0.0167)	(0.0192)	(0.0193)	(0.0195)
HISPANIC	0.2836 ***	0.0968 ***	0.1098 ***	0.1384 ***
	(0.0254)	(0.0230)	(0.0298)	(0.0205)
PMOS_I1	−0.0258	0.4853 ***	0.3198 ***	0.3835 ***
	(0.0261)	(0.0331)	(0.0267)	(0.0306)

Table D.6—continued

Variable	Army	Navy	Air Force	Marine Corps
PMOS_I2	0.0261	0.4746 ***	0.2999 ***	0.2444 ***
	(0.0274)	(0.0315)	(0.0307)	(0.0267)
PMOS_I3	0.1755 ***	0.4253 ***	0.3835 ***	
	(0.0254)	(0.0336)	(0.0276)	
PMOS_I4	0.1535 ***	0.4589 ***	0.0518	0.2790 ***
	(0.0417)	(0.0688)	(0.0350)	(0.0472)
PMOS_I5	0.2221 ***	0.3166 ***	0.4248 ***	0.4207 ***
	(0.0241)	(0.0313)	(0.0239)	(0.0221)
PMOS_I6	–0.0315	0.0892 ***	0.3473 ***	0.2825 ***
	(0.0244)	(0.0269)	(0.0224)	(0.0209)
PMOS_I7	–0.0783 **	–0.0574	0.1779 ***	0.1725 ***
	(0.0374)	(0.0365)	(0.0324)	(0.0392)
PMOS_I8	0.0249	0.2072 ***	0.1857 ***	0.1800 ***
	(0.0262)	(0.0376)	(0.0285)	(0.0210)
UNEPLY_A	–0.1236 ***	0.0282 **	–0.4067 ***	
	(0.0104)	(0.0142)	(0.0098)	
UNEPLY_R	0.4841 ***	0.4084 ***	0.3015 ***	
	(0.0394)	(0.0428)	(0.0383)	
ETS97	0.3026 ***	0.1002 ***	–0.0373 *	0.0601 ***
	(0.0217)	(0.0253)	(0.0218)	(0.0192)
ETS98	0.4141 ***	0.4528 ***	–0.1659 ***	0.0625 ***
	(0.0395)	(0.0436)	(0.0387)	(0.0195)
ETS99	0.4020 ***	0.4735 ***	–0.3901 ***	0.0377 **
	(0.0500)	(0.0550)	(0.0484)	(0.0192)

NOTE: Standard errors in parentheses. *** = significant at 0.01, ** = significant at 0.05, * = significant at 0.10.

Table D.7

**Tobit/Probit Model of Time to E-5 Promotion and Reenlistment:
First Term**

Variable	Army	Navy	Air Force	Marine Corps
Time to E-5				
Constant	79.0260 ***	14.4412 ***	92.0762 ***	72.4699 ***
	(0.5788)	(0.1019)	(0.8376)	(0.2640)
N1_	−2.4963 ***	−0.4191 ***	−2.5776 ***	−0.2699 ***
	(0.2038)	(0.0458)	(0.2842)	(0.0993)
N2_	−4.8638 ***	−0.4073 ***	−3.3523 ***	−0.6574 ***
	(0.3389)	(0.0482)	(0.5666)	(0.1280)
N3_	−7.0300 ***	−0.5805 ***	−3.4793 ***	−1.5251 ***
	(0.7017)	(0.0542)	(1.2606)	(0.1926)
H1_	−0.3363	0.0767 **	−0.9036 ***	−0.9035 ***
	(0.2229)	(0.0380)	(0.2911)	(0.1093)
H2_	0.6530	0.1336 ***	−0.7276	−0.7189 ***
	(0.4427)	(0.0503)	(0.4764)	(0.1959)
H3_	1.7086 *	−0.1507	−0.8575	−0.9924 **
	(1.0138)	(0.1255)	(0.6019)	(0.4804)
AFQTI_II	−4.2657 ***	−2.6159 ***	−11.3531 ***	−0.8294 ***
	(0.2680)	(0.0542)	(0.4027)	(0.1185)
AFQTIIIA	−1.8571 ***	−1.2857 ***	−3.8293 ***	−0.3886 ***
	(0.2746)	(0.0548)	(0.4338)	(0.1249)
AFQTIV	4.3763 ***	0.6708 *	3.7651	0.0580
	(0.9968)	(0.3616)	(4.9253)	(1.3257)
AFQTMISS	−3.5764 ***	−2.2430 ***	−8.2319 ***	−0.6016 ***
	(0.5239)	(0.0909)	(0.7797)	(0.2197)
GED_	2.3292 ***	0.3731 ***	0.0000	0.3416
	(0.6407)	(0.1231)		(0.2664)
NHSG_	−1.0196	0.7317 ***	0.0000	0.6796
	(1.9144)	(0.2258)		(1.7819)
SPSS_	−7.7190 ***	−1.3496 ***	−1.2233 **	−1.7899 ***
	(0.4268)	(0.1328)	(0.5749)	(0.3522)
E4P25	−14.0700 ***		3.9738 ***	−21.3550 ***
	(0.4228)		(0.4920)	(0.1777)
E4P50	−8.6137 ***	−0.3758	0.1014	−15.1257 ***
	(0.4148)	(0.2990)	(0.5476)	(0.1799)
E4P75	−5.5581 ***		1.6865 ***	−9.2692 ***
	(0.6115)		(0.5252)	(0.1869)

Table D.7—continued

Variable	Army	Navy	Air Force	Marine Corps
PMOS_I1_	4.4979 ***	−1.1040 ***	2.2076 ***	0.6098 ***
	(0.3642)	(0.0878)	(0.6679)	(0.1657)
PMOS_I2_	−0.1267	−1.9755 ***	3.2808 ***	−1.5412 ***
	(0.3669)	(0.0834)	(0.4546)	(0.1631)
PMOS_I3_	6.7906 ***	2.5940 ***	2.9830 ***	
	(0.3333)	(0.0974)	(0.4480)	
PMOS_I4_	−1.9248 ***	−1.4233 ***	5.6860 ***	−3.5548 ***
	(0.5363)	(0.1537)	(0.7226)	(0.2630)
PMOS_I5_	4.5219 ***	−0.6485 ***	1.9280 ***	2.1087 ***
	(0.3201)	(0.0823)	(0.5786)	(0.1391)
PMOS_I6_	6.4390 ***	0.2127 ***	0.3225	−0.2436 *
	(0.3453)	(0.0727)	(0.2654)	(0.1280)
PMOS_I7_	4.8972 ***	−0.9112 ***	1.5648 ***	1.4110 ***
	(0.5330)	(0.0919)	(0.3382)	(0.2651)
PMOS_I8_	3.7661 ***	1.4425 ***	3.1178 ***	1.8103 ***
	(0.3631)	(0.1029)	(0.4861)	(0.1511)
ETS97_	−1.5512 ***	0.7138 ***	0.6051 ***	−0.3998 ***
	(0.2353)	(0.0491)	(0.1627)	(0.1277)
ETS98_	−1.4862 ***	0.7102 ***	0.9408 ***	−1.8459 ***
	(0.2595)	(0.0534)	(0.2167)	(0.1321)
ETS99_	−1.4415 ***	0.5537 ***	0.1511	−3.6736 ***
	(0.2921)	(0.0563)	(0.1151)	(0.1358)
ACQ2	0.8997 ***	−0.0468 *	−12.1567 ***	−0.2042
	(0.2552)	(0.0269)	(2.4525)	(0.1298)
ACQ3	1.2248 ***	−0.0365	0.5991 ***	−0.0184
	(0.2305)	(0.0266)	(0.0681)	(0.1191)
ACQ4	−0.3963	0.0648 **	0.8269 ***	−0.0432
	(0.2493)	(0.0294)	(0.1070)	(0.1251)
Reenlistment				
Const2	−3.8520 ***	4.1126 ***	0.7363 ***	0.4590 ***
	(0.1892)	(1.1651)	(0.1785)	(0.0428)
N1	0.2924 ***	−0.1402 ***	0.1315 ***	0.0335 ***
	(0.0119)	(0.0345)	(0.0420)	(0.0125)
N2	0.4876 ***	−0.1458 ***	0.0677	0.0625 ***
	(0.0212)	(0.0376)	(0.0603)	(0.0158)
N3	0.6306 ***	−0.0865 *	0.1432 *	0.1439 ***
	(0.0447)	(0.0472)	(0.0767)	(0.0237)

Table D.7—continued

Variable	Army	Navy	Air Force	Marine Corps
H1	0.1653 ***	−0.0370 *	1.1736 ***	−0.0111
	(0.0127)	(0.0218)	(0.3048)	(0.0135)
H2	0.1541 ***	0.0359	0.3757 ***	−0.0433 *
	(0.0250)	(0.0286)	(0.1137)	(0.0228)
H3	0.1797 ***	0.1038	−0.3795	−0.0894
	(0.0553)	(0.0690)	(0.5995)	(0.0622)
AFQTI_II	−0.0073	−1.4011 ***	0.9378 ***	−0.0233 *
	(0.0165)	(0.2109)	(0.2395)	(0.0138)
AFQTIIIA	0.0223	−0.7261 ***	−0.0033	0.0104
	(0.0157)	(0.1073)	(0.1659)	(0.0141)
AFQTIV	−0.0719	0.6494 ***	0.8280	−0.0020
	(0.0525)	(0.2112)	(0.6377)	(0.1324)
AFQTMISS	0.0618 **	−1.0153 ***	1.0382 ***	−0.0393
	(0.0293)	(0.1859)	(0.0739)	(0.0241)
GED	0.0578	0.2822 ***	0.1887 ***	0.0636 **
	(0.0354)	(0.0751)	(0.0223)	(0.0300)
NHSG	−0.0706	0.5156 ***	0.4903 ***	0.1702
	(0.0898)	(0.1368)	(0.0218)	(0.1939)
SPSS	−0.0433	−0.6711 ***	1.7466 ***	−0.2026 ***
	(0.0280)	(0.1270)	(0.0376)	(0.0449)
FEMALE	0.1326 ***	−0.1352 ***	0.0012	0.0761 ***
	(0.0136)	(0.0154)	(0.0125)	(0.0244)
BLACK	0.4192 ***	0.4893 ***	0.4057 ***	0.4251 ***
	(0.0125)	(0.0139)	(0.0145)	(0.0152)
HISPANIC	0.2271 ***	0.1007 ***	0.0752 ***	0.1338 ***
	(0.0194)	(0.0167)	(0.0240)	(0.0163)
DEPEND	0.2113 ***	0.3888 ***	0.2171 ***	0.3264 ***
	(0.0099)	(0.0103)	(0.0097)	(0.0109)
PMOS_I1	−0.0412 **	−0.0971	−0.1797	0.3949 ***
	(0.0205)	(0.1011)	(0.1236)	(0.0230)
PMOS_I2	0.0259	−0.6116 ***	0.3413 ***	0.2003 ***
	(0.0205)	(0.1641)	(0.0679)	(0.0201)
PMOS_I3	0.1151 ***	1.7849 ***	0.1106	
	(0.0212)	(0.2157)	(0.0798)	
PMOS_I4	0.1992 ***	−0.2579 *	−0.1536	0.2378 ***
	(0.0318)	(0.1435)	(0.1011)	(0.0338)

Table D.7—continued

Variable	Army	Navy	Air Force	Marine Corps
PMOS_I5	0.1668 ***	−0.0447	0.0480	0.4890 ***
	(0.0192)	(0.0696)	(0.1046)	(0.0170)
PMOS_I6	−0.0598 ***	0.2378 ***	−0.0412	0.2922 ***
	(0.0204)	(0.0439)	(0.0969)	(0.0158)
PMOS_I7	−0.0362	−0.4942 ***	−0.3655 **	0.2276 ***
	(0.0304)	(0.0897)	(0.1751)	(0.0305)
PMOS_I8	0.0344	1.0178 ***	0.0045	0.2241 ***
	(0.0209)	(0.1275)	(0.0875)	(0.0167)
UNEPLY_A	−0.2035 ***	0.0200 *	−0.4977 ***	
	(0.0083)	(0.0106)	(0.0078)	
UNEPLY_R	0.7314 ***	0.4487 ***	0.6572 ***	
	(0.0292)	(0.0310)	(0.0303)	
ETS97	0.3978 ***	0.5171 ***	−0.0322	0.1203 ***
	(0.0170)	(0.0649)	(0.0365)	(0.0149)
ETS98	0.5914 ***	0.8722 ***	−0.2289 ***	0.1047 ***
	(0.0297)	(0.0707)	(0.0633)	(0.0149)
ETS99	0.6254 ***	0.8461 ***	−0.7996 ***	0.0656 ***
	(0.0374)	(0.0660)	(0.1024)	(0.0148)
SigmaE	18.0881 ***	3.2534 ***	14.8882 ***	8.3903 ***
	(0.1397)	(0.0302)	(0.1383)	(0.0385)
SigmaE2	1.0000	1.0000	1.0000	1.0000
Rho	−0.3460 ***	−0.3234 ***	−0.0661 ***	−0.2894 ***
	(0.0072)	(0.0084)	(0.0146)	(0.0063)
Gamma	0.0091 ***	−0.5374 ***	0.1153 ***	−0.0328 ***
	(0.0012)	(0.0802)	(0.0265)	(0.0007)

NOTE: Standard errors in parentheses. *** = significant at 0.01, ** = significant at 0.05, * = significant at 0.10.

Table D.8

Tobit/Probit Model of Time to E-5 Promotion and Reenlistment: Second Term

Variable	Army	Navy	Air Force	Marine Corps
Time to E-5				
Constant	75.2282 ***	13.3975 ***	60.4898 ***	71.4693 ***
	(1.3861)	(0.1202)	(0.4739)	(1.8661)
N1_	−1.6812 ***	−1.1380 ***	−1.2766 ***	−0.6597 ***
	(0.2600)	(0.0605)	(0.1803)	(0.2544)
N2_	−1.6132 ***	−1.6216 ***	−1.1084 ***	−2.1176 ***
	(0.4289)	(0.0814)	(0.3301)	(0.3472)
N3_	−2.4687 **	−1.6118 ***	−2.3763 ***	−1.9937 ***
	(1.0151)	(0.1008)	(0.6473)	(0.5855)
H1_	1.0685 ***	−0.6703 ***	0.6336 ***	−2.8196 ***
	(0.2873)	(0.0578)	(0.1765)	(0.3283)
H2_	1.9146 ***	−0.8614 ***	0.9453 ***	−2.6659 ***
	(0.5901)	(0.1086)	(0.3080)	(0.7562)
H3_	7.5347 ***	−0.8376 ***	2.3039 ***	−3.4619 **
	(1.3658)	(0.3156)	(0.3694)	(1.7441)
AFQTI_II	−4.0863 ***	−1.7053 ***	−4.1528 ***	−1.8234 ***
	(0.2878)	(0.0744)	(0.2068)	(0.3062)
AFQTIIIA	−2.1847 ***	−0.8429 ***	−0.7293 ***	−0.8793 ***
	(0.2849)	(0.0690)	(0.2157)	(0.2972)
AFQTIV	4.8053 ***	1.0203 ***	5.0194 ***	1.8463
	(0.6915)	(0.0792)	(1.5387)	(2.6204)
AFQTMISS	−5.2173 ***	−1.4294 ***	−6.1851 ***	−3.2536 **
	(0.8675)	(0.1170)	(0.6161)	(1.4405)
GED_	3.3155 ***	0.2866 **	0.0000	0.5134
	(0.6683)	(0.1437)		(0.6356)
NHSG_	2.0464	0.1932	0.0000	2.7026
	(1.7666)	(0.1786)		(3.2928)
SPSS_	−5.8628 ***	−0.4713 ***	3.1078 ***	−1.5954
	(0.7814)	(0.1523)	(0.3022)	(1.3093)
E4P25	−10.9021 ***		2.2532 ***	−21.2812 ***
	(1.2737)		(0.3355)	(1.7682)
E4P50	−4.4769 ***	−0.8869 ***	1.0000 ***	−9.1697 ***
	(1.3784)	(0.0531)	(0.3547)	(1.8583)
E4P75	1.2598		1.4082 ***	−6.7316 ***
	(2.5921)		(0.3524)	(1.9843)

Table D.8—continued

Variable	Army	Navy	Air Force	Marine Corps
PMOS_I1_	3.7564 ***	−0.8910 ***	−0.1134	2.0820 ***
	(0.5039)	(0.1310)	(0.4356)	(0.5727)
PMOS_I2_	−2.0442 ***	−1.7220 ***	1.6162 ***	1.8310 ***
	(0.4711)	(0.1248)	(0.3007)	(0.5227)
PMOS_I3_	5.0581 ***	0.7054 ***	1.9983 ***	
	(0.4329)	(0.1034)	(0.2957)	
PMOS_I4_	−3.3358 ***	−1.3497 ***	1.3684 ***	−4.8485 ***
	(0.7689)	(0.2262)	(0.4094)	(0.9104)
PMOS_I5_	2.7487 ***	−1.4018 ***	−0.3312	0.6167
	(0.3707)	(0.1076)	(0.3868)	(0.3831)
PMOS_I6_	5.2638 ***	0.0419	4.4081 ***	0.2631
	(0.3765)	(0.0882)	(0.2212)	(0.3984)
PMOS_I7_	0.6670	−0.2209 *	7.9269 ***	0.1135
	(0.8341)	(0.1224)	(0.2211)	(0.7108)
PMOS_I8_	1.9988 ***	1.5396 ***	12.7747 ***	1.9356 ***
	(0.4002)	(0.1054)	(0.2228)	(0.4000)
ETS97_	−2.2499 ***	−0.0125	0.5312 **	−1.9404 ***
	(0.4745)	(0.0790)	(0.2112)	(0.4622)
ETS98_	−4.1497 ***	0.0907	1.2346 ***	−2.0408 ***
	(0.4880)	(0.0785)	(0.2099)	(0.4268)
ETS99_	−2.5473 ***	0.2324 ***	−2.4238 ***	−1.5600 ***
	(0.5017)	(0.0773)	(0.1895)	(0.4403)
ACQ2	0.7555 **	0.0598	0.6840	−0.1316
	(0.3442)	(0.0776)	(0.5202)	(0.3452)
ACQ3	1.0817 ***	−0.1803 ***	0.1735 ***	0.1341
	(0.3060)	(0.0697)	(0.0143)	(0.3318)
ACQ4	−0.5030	0.1115	0.1695 ***	0.0976
	(0.3188)	(0.0727)	(0.0261)	(0.3701)
Reenlistment				
Const2	−0.6661 *	−1.0254 ***	0.1977 ***	−1.1041 ***
	(0.3534)	(0.3239)	(0.0486)	(0.2729)
N1	0.2041 ***	0.3115 ***	0.0904 ***	0.2719 ***
	(0.0171)	(0.0227)	(0.0139)	(0.0401)
N2	0.1997 ***	0.3329 ***	0.1266 ***	0.4998 ***
	(0.0255)	(0.0316)	(0.0229)	(0.0537)
N3	0.2112 ***	0.5912 ***	0.1296 ***	0.7984 ***
	(0.0555)	(0.0394)	(0.0286)	(0.0829)

Table D.8—continued

Variable	Army	Navy	Air Force	Marine Corps
H1	0.1766 ***	0.1836 ***	0.0499 **	0.3102 ***
	(0.0181)	(0.0214)	(0.0214)	(0.0528)
H2	0.2132 ***	0.4122 ***	0.0662 ***	0.5801 ***
	(0.0340)	(0.0372)	(0.0169)	(0.1107)
H3	0.0197	0.5333 ***	−0.2707 **	0.5192
	(0.0749)	(0.0954)	(0.1180)	(0.3889)
AFQTI_II	−0.0244	0.0675 **	0.1794 ***	0.1489 ***
	(0.0255)	(0.0321)	(0.0535)	(0.0481)
AFQTIIIA	0.0102	0.0047	0.3298	0.1392 ***
	(0.0205)	(0.0256)	(0.3006)	(0.0465)
AFQTIV	−0.1230 ***	−0.0669 **	0.8280	−0.0484
	(0.0471)	(0.0307)	(0.0000)	(0.4057)
AFQTMISS	0.1901 ***	0.2243 ***	0.0419	0.3543 *
	(0.0576)	(0.0438)	(0.0257)	(0.1845)
GED	−0.0267	−0.1196 **	−0.4006	−0.1084
	(0.0428)	(0.0472)	(0.4165)	(0.0933)
NHSG	−0.0388	−0.1637 ***	−0.1170	−0.8400
	(0.1155)	(0.0572)	(0.4210)	(0.7994)
SPSS	0.0410	0.0803	0.0664	−0.1380
	(0.0473)	(0.0530)	(0.5576)	(0.1293)
FEMALE	0.0843 ***	−0.0758 ***	−0.0848 ***	−0.0721
	(0.0223)	(0.0248)	(0.0147)	(0.0694)
BLACK	0.2681 ***	0.1303 ***	0.1591 ***	0.2550 ***
	(0.0166)	(0.0195)	(0.0156)	(0.0438)
HISPANIC	0.0729 **	0.0507 *	0.0937 ***	0.1081 *
	(0.0299)	(0.0290)	(0.0293)	(0.0577)
DEPEND	0.1714 ***	0.0925 ***	0.0760 ***	0.0813 *
	(0.0186)	(0.0206)	(0.0133)	(0.0458)
PMOS_I1	0.0121	0.3839 ***	0.0180	−0.1295
	(0.0340)	(0.0435)	(0.0275)	(0.0922)
PMOS_I2	0.0762 **	0.1360 ***	−0.0726 **	0.0737
	(0.0297)	(0.0439)	(0.0288)	(0.0800)
PMOS_I3	0.2510 ***	0.4594 ***	0.1162 ***	
	(0.0358)	(0.0382)	(0.0288)	
PMOS_I4	0.3132 ***	0.2202 ***	−0.0140	0.2990 **
	(0.0493)	(0.0762)	(0.0343)	(0.1263)

Table D.8—continued

Variable	Army	Navy	Air Force	Marine Corps
PMOS_I5	0.2841 ***	0.2932 ***	0.1684 ***	0.0845
	(0.0277)	(0.0393)	(0.0247)	(0.0598)
PMOS_I6	0.0877 ***	0.0358	0.1441 ***	0.0017
	(0.0317)	(0.0304)	(0.0244)	(0.0609)
PMOS_I7	0.1796 ***	0.1740 ***	0.1099 ***	0.1204
	(0.0500)	(0.0433)	(0.0327)	(0.1133)
PMOS_I8	0.0230	−0.0680	0.1689 ***	0.0235
	(0.0269)	(0.0424)	(0.0302)	(0.0625)
UNEPLY_A	0.0963 ***	0.1531 ***	0.0422 ***	
	(0.0104)	(0.0132)	(0.0088)	
UNEPLY_R	−0.0026	0.0438	−0.0338	
	(0.0419)	(0.0509)	(0.0326)	
ETS97	0.5650 ***	0.0314	−0.0150	0.1028 *
	(0.0302)	(0.0322)	(0.0249)	(0.0608)
ETS98	0.4043 ***	0.0085	0.0043	0.0175
	(0.0477)	(0.0528)	(0.0436)	(0.0567)
ETS99	0.3722 ***	0.0723	−0.0525	−0.4701 ***
	(0.0548)	(0.0640)	(0.0612)	(0.0590)
SigmaE	17.6566 ***	3.3798 ***	14.8699 ***	8.6586 ***
	(0.1384)	(0.0293)	(0.0745)	(0.0754)
SigmaE2	1.0000	1.0000	1.0000	1.0000
Rho	−0.4921 ***	−0.4366 ***	−0.4810 ***	−0.2214 ***
	(0.0070)	(0.0083)	(0.0049)	(0.0176)
Gamma	−0.0116 ***	−0.0380 ***	−0.0062 *	0.0185 ***
	(0.0040)	(0.0111)	(0.0036)	(0.0053)

NOTE: Standard errors in parentheses. *** = significant at 0.01, ** = significant at 0.05, * = significant at 0.10.

GLOSSARY OF VARIABLES

The following list defines the variables used in Appendixes C and D.

NOTE: Variables followed by an underscore are measured as of the time of promotion instead of the time of reenlistment.

Main Effect Deployment Indicators

Reference category: No nonhostile episodes.

N1	1 nonhostile deployment
N2	2 nonhostile deployments
N3	3 or more nonhostile deployments

Reference category: No deployment with hostile component.

H1	1 deployment with a hostile component
H2	2 deployments with hostile components
H3	3 or more deployments with hostile components

Interacted Deployment Indicators

Reference category: No episodes of either type.

N1H0	1 nonhostile deployment 0 with hostile component
N2H0	2 nonhostile deployments 0 with hostile component

N3H0	3 or more nonhostile deployments 0 with hostile component
N0H1	0 nonhostile deployments 1 with hostile component
N1H1	1 nonhostile deployment 1 with hostile component
N2H1	2 nonhostile deployments 1 with hostile component
N3H1	3 or more nonhostile deployments 1 with hostile component
N0H2	0 nonhostile deployments 2 with hostile component
N1H2	1 nonhostile deployment 2 with hostile component
N2H2	2 nonhostile deployments 2 with hostile component
N3H2	3 or more nonhostile deployments 2 with hostile component
N0H3	0 nonhostile deployments 3 or more with hostile component
N1H3	1 nonhostile deployment 3 or more with hostile component
N2H3	2 nonhostile deployments 3 or more with hostile component
N3H3	3 or more nonhostile deployments 3 or more with hostile component

Promotion Speed

E4P25	Indicates member made E-4 as fast or faster than 25 percent of entry cohort
E4P50	Indicates member made E-4 as fast or faster than 50 percent of entry cohort
E4P75	Indicates member made E-4 as fast or faster than 75 percent of entry cohort

Test Scores
Reference category: AFQT IIIB (31st to 49th percentile).

AFQTI_II	Armed Forces Qualification Test score category I (93rd percentile and higher) or II (65th to 93rd percentile)
AFQTIIIA	AFQT IIIA (50th to 64th percentile)
AFQTIV	AFQT IV (11th to 30th percentile)
AFQTMISS	Missing AFQT score

Education
Reference category: High school graduate.

GED	General Equivalency Diploma holder
NHSG	Non–high school graduate without GED
SPSS	Some post-secondary school

Dependents

DEPEND	Indicates 1 or more dependents

Occupation
Reference category: Infantry gun crews and seamanship specialists.

PMOS_I1	Electronic equipment repairers
PMOS_I2	Communications and intelligence specialists
PMOS_I3	Medical and dental specialists
PMOS_I4	Other technical and allied specialists
PMOS_I5	Functional support and administration
PMOS_I6	Electrical/mechanical equipment repairers
PMOS_I7	Craftsmen
PMOS_I8	Service and supply handlers

Unemployment Rate

UNEPLY_A   National unemployment rate at time of accession

UNEPLY_R   National unemployment rate at time of reenlistment decision

Decision Time

Reference category: Decisions in FY1996.

ETS97   Expiration of term of service or decision fell in FY1997

ETS98   ETS or decision fell in FY1998

ETS99   ETS or decision fell in FY1999

Accession Quarter

Reference category: First calendar quarter.

ACQ2   Second calendar quarter

ACQ3   Third calendar quarter

ACQ4   Fourth calendar quarter

Other

Sigma E   Standard deviation of time to E-5 promotion

Sigma E2   Standard deviation of propensity to reenlist (constrained to equal 1)

Rho   Correlation coefficient between the error terms in the time–to–E-5–promotion equation and the reenlistment equation

Gamma   Coefficient on the variable for expected time to E-5 promotion in the reenlistment equation

REFERENCES

Asch, Beth J., and John T. Warner, *A Theory of Military Compensation and Personnel Policy*, Santa Monica, Calif.: RAND, MR-439-OSD, 1994.

Buddin, Richard, Daniel Levy, Janet Hanley, and Donald Waldman, *Promotion Tempo and Enlisted Retention*, Santa Monica, Calif.: RAND, R-4135-FMP, 1992.

Crawley, Vince, "Hardship-Duty, Imminent-Danger Pays Overlap," *Army Times*, November 26, 2001, p. 12.

Fricker, Ronald D., Jr., *The Effects of Perstempo on Officer Retention in the U.S. Military*, Santa Monica, Calif.: RAND, MR-1556-OSD, 2002.

General Accounting Office (GAO), *Quality of Life for U.S. Soldiers Deployed in the Balkans*, Washington, D.C.: GAO, GAO-01-201R, December 14, 2000.

Gotz, Glenn A., and John J. McCall, *A Dynamic Retention Model for Air Force Officers: Theory and Estimates*, R-3028-AF, 1984.

Hosek, James, and Mark Totten, *Does Perstempo Hurt Reenlistment? The Effect of Long or Hostile Perstempo on Reenlistment*, Santa Monica, Calif.: RAND, MR-990-OSD, 1998.

Office of the Secretary of Defense, *Military Compensation Background Papers: Compensation Elements and Related Manpower Cost Items, Their Purposes and Legislative Backgrounds*, Fifth Edition, Department of Defense, September 1996. [This document is also referred to as the "White Book."]

Sortor, Ronald E., and J. Michael Polich, *Deployments and Army Personnel Tempo*, Santa Monica, Calif.: RAND, MR-1417-A, 2001.

Tiemeyer, Peter, Casey Wardynski, and Richard Buddin, *Financial Management Problems Among Enlisted Personnel*, Santa Monica, Calif.: RAND, DB-241-OSD, 1999.

Under Secretary of Defense (Comptroller), *Military Pay Policy and Precedures: Active Duty and Reserve Pay*, Volume 7A, updated June 5, 2001. Available online at www.dtic.mil/comptroller/fmr/07a (last accessed July 17, 2002).

Wardynski, E. Casey, *Military Compensation in the Age of Two-Income Households: Adding Spouses' Earnings to the Compensation Policy Mix*, Santa Monica, Calif.: RAND, RGSD-154, 2000.

Williamson, Stephanie, *A Description of U.S. Enlisted Personnel Promotion Systems*, Santa Monica, Calif.: RAND, MR-1067-OSD, 1999.